ILEX FOUNDATION SERIES 26

NAQQALI TRILOGY

Also in the Ilex Foundation Series

NAQQALI TRILOGY

Bahram Beyzaie

Translated and with an Introduction by

Richard Saul Chason
Nikta Sabouri

Ilex Foundation
Boston, Massachusetts

Distributed by Harvard University Press
Cambridge, Massachusetts and London, England

Naqqali Trilogy
by Bahram Beyzaie
Translated and with an introduction by Richard Saul Chason and Nikta Sabouri

Copyright © 2022 Ilex Foundation
All Rights Reserved

Published by Ilex Foundation, Boston, Massachusetts

Distributed by Harvard University Press, Cambridge, Massachusetts and London, England

Production editor: Christopher Dadian
Cover design: Joni Godlove
Printed in the United States of America

Cover image: Relief from Sasanian silver and gilt dish. 5th–6th century. Cleveland Museum of Art.

Library of Congress Cataloging-in-Publication Data

Names: Bayẕā'ī, Bahrām, author. | Chason, Richard Saul, translator. |
Sabouri, Nikta, translator.
Title: Naqqali trilogy / Bahram Beyzaie ; translated and with an
introduction by Richard Saul Chason, Nikta Sabouri.
Description: Boston, Massachusetts : Ilex Foundation, [2022] | Series: Ilex
Foundation series ; 26 | Azhdahak -- Arash -- Testament of Bondar
Bidakhsh. | Summary: "Blending modes of traditional Iranian storytelling
and mythological ritual with contemporary dramatic philosophy and
technique, the Naqqali Trilogy is a cycle of three works of mythological
revisionism. It celebrates a renaissance of Persian cultural tradition
while reframing ancient tales into a modern psychodrama of outcasts and
oppression in a land of tyranny and injustice. This volume also includes
a detailed introduction that provides background information on Beyzaie,
the mythological basis of the plays, the nature of the plays in
performance, and on the plays' distinctive employ of the Persian
language and the replication of the dramatic prose poetry into an
English equivalent"-- Provided by publisher.
Identifiers: LCCN 2022052161 | ISBN 9780674292390 (paperback)
Subjects: LCSH: Bayẕā'ī, Bahrām--Translations into English. | LCGFT:
Drama.
Classification: LCC PK6561.B4 N36 2022 | DDC 891/.5523--dc23/eng/20221125
LC record available at https://lccn.loc.gov/2022052161

for Richard Saul Chason's parents,
Maureen Barry and Mark Chason

for Nikta Sabouri's grandmother, parents,
sister, and husband, Hani Bakhshaee

Contents

Acknowledgments

We would like to acknowledge the invaluable support for the production of this book of Mojdeh Shamsaie, Abbas Milani, Mohammad Batmanglij, Lloyd Schwartz, Michael Feingold, Rana Esfandiary, Shahla Haeri, Marjan Moosavi, Jani Monet Rodrigues, Parastou Eslami, Niloo Fotouhi, Amin Feizpour, Asma Khoshmehr, Q-mars Haeri, Kelley Holley, Andrew Child, and Roma Parhad.

Introduction

Richard Saul Chason
Nikta Sabouri

BAHRAM BEYZAIE is widely regarded as the Shakespeare of Persia, yet he remains largely unknown to the English-speaking world. Born in 1938 in Tehran to a family of poets and literary scholars, Beyzaie has become not only the most influential and celebrated of all Iranian dramatists but also an acclaimed filmmaker, theater director, and scholar of Iranian and Eastern theater, with over seventy books, monographs, plays, and screenplays to his credit. His 1965 treatise, *Theatre in Iran*, remains the definitive history of Iranian theater. His ten features and four short films stand among the finest and most beloved of the Iranian New Wave cinema. And yet, whether it be for the difficulty of translating his work into English or for the socio-political forces that impact cultural exchange between the worlds of Farsi and of English, very little of Beyzaie's work has yet been made available in English despite his acclaim and cultural significance.

At the time of this writing, only a small handful of the writer's prolific dramatic writings have been translated into English.[1] In this volume, we present translations of three foundational works in Beyzaie's oeuvre, masterpieces of world drama in complete English translation for the first time. *Naqqali Trilogy* consists of three works of mythological revisionism that blend traditional Iranian storytelling modes with contemporary Western theatrical practice: *Arash* (1957), *Azhdahak* (1959), and *Testament of Bondar Bidakhsh* (1961, revised 1997). Each of these works, despite being overtly theatrical texts written for live performance, may appear more like prose short stories to one degree or another, and so a broad understanding of the traditional Persian theater Beyzaie echoes in the trilogy may provide insight into their inherent dramatic quality.

Despite the rich cultural abundance of poetry, literature, music, and dance throughout several thousand years of Perisan history, until the twentieth century

---

1. These include Beyzaie's Puppet Play Trilogy in *Modern Persian Drama: An Anthology*, ed. Gisele Kapuscinski (University Press of America, 1987); *The Marrionettes* and *Four Boxes* in *Iranian Drama: An Anthology*, ed, M.R. Ghanoonparvar and John Green (Mazda, 1989); *Death of Yadzgerd*, trans. Manuchehr Anvar (Bisheh, 2022); *Death of the King* and *Arash* (in abridged and adapted form) in *Stories from the Rains of Love and Death: Four Plays from Iran*, trans. Soheil Parsa with Peter Farbridge and Brian Quirt (Playwrights Canada Press, 2008); *Memoirs of the Actor in a Supporting Role*, trans. Mohammad R. Ghanoonparvar (Mazda, 2010); and *Kalat Claimed*, trans. Manuchehr Anvar (Bisheh, 2022).

1

Iran lacked a significant tradition of theater, or at least of theater in the Western mode of dramas composed by a playwright and performed in a playhouse. Iran's history of oppressive rule through the ages could not foster a culture of theater, which generally demands significant popular and commercial support for free or cultivated artistic expression, even in monarchical societies. However, despite an absence of plays at court or in publicly-supported civic spaces, as there was in ancient Greece and Rome, Iran certainly produced a rich array of traditional folk theater. Traditional Iranian theatrical forms include *naqqali*, a style of coffeehouse storytelling, *Ta'zieh*, a religious ceremonial practice bearing similarities to French medieval mystery plays, *kheimah shah bazi*, puppet theater, *saye-bazi*, shadow puppetry, *ru howzi*, comic folk drama, and a host of variations on these forms.

Beyzaie was one of a generation of Persian dramatists in the mid-twentieth century who brought to Iran its first fertile period of dramatic literature, joining such voices as Gholamhoseyn Sa'edi, Abbas Na'lbandian, Akbar Radi, Ali Nassirian, Bijan Mofid, Sadeq Chubak, Nader Ebrahimi, and Mahmud Rahbar. Beyzaie, however, was distinguished among the artists of his generation as the first and most prominent dramatist to blend traditional Iranian theatrical forms with a Western dramatic mode.

The plays of the *Naqqali Trilogy* specifically incorporate elements of *naqqali*, a traditional, theatrical form of storytelling performed by individual storytellers, or *naqqal*s, often in coffeehouses. *Naqqal*s recite, frequently through song, stories of Persian mythology. They use largely as the basis of their stories the *Shahnameh*, or the Persian Book of Kings, an eleventh-century work of epic poetry by Abolqasem Ferdowsi. A chronology of pre-Islamic Persia from the dawn of humanity through the Arab conquest of Iran in the seventh century CE, the *Shahnameh* blends mythology and history in spectacular heroic verse and serves as the national epic of Persia, and also as one of the authoritative sources of Persian myth utilized by later artists.

Of note, while traditional *naqqali* derives its stories largely from the *Shahnameh*, Beyzaie also incorporates into his plays elements of the *Avesta* and of other sacred texts of Zoroastrianism (the religion of pre-Islamic Persia, whose mythology was the basis of Ferdowsi's work), and of Sanskrit works including the India epic *Mahabharata*, which draws upon a cognate Indo-Iranian mythological tradition.

And yet the influence of *naqqali* on the three plays in Beyzaie's trilogy is striking and overt. The works appear at first glance less as dialogue-driven dramas and more as bodies of prose for narrative storytelling. One could easily imagine the texts set to music, or illustrated with a backdrop representing the action of each scene, as in a variation of *naqqali* practice called *pardeh-khani*. And while all three works could be staged in a more-or-less traditional manner of a *naqqali* performance, they also each contain elements of contemporary Western dramatic technique resonating in a decided dramatic modernity.

For one, while the plays use ancient myths as the basis of their plots and characters, all three plays serve as radical acts of mythological revisionism, recasting ancient figures as outcasts oppressed by civilizations of tyranny. Beyzaie adapts the figures in each play to reflect the psychological torment of life under the oppressive regimes of modern Iran, merging familiar archetypes with the experience of the modern world to create writing that is at once ancient in form and psychologically contemporary in content. In fact, Beyzaie refers to the form of these plays not strictly as *naqqali* but as *barkhani*, a term the artist invented that translates roughly to "recitation." For the figures in *Naqqali Trilogy* are not simply storytellers but living characters with modern psychological depth, and the performers of the plays must weave between a style of performative storytelling and inner psychological realism, blending ancient and contemporary theatricality to create a renaissance of form and exaltation.

It must be noted that Beyzaie's blending of the ancient and the contemporary rests not only in the content of the dramas but also in his distinctive use of the Persian language. Before the Arab conquest of Persia in the seventh century CE, the people of Iran spoke Middle Persian, or Pahlavi, essentially a collection of dialects of the Persian language that varied widely throughout the kingdom. Once Islam was brought upon Persia, the new ruling caliphs engendered religious and cultural unity through the destruction of Zoroastrian writing and cultural landmarks, replacing Zoroastrian practice with that dictated by new Islamic doctrine. As part of the destruction of pre-Islamic Persia, Middle Persian was unified and blended with Arabic to become contemporary Farsi.

Beyzaie, in an attempt to introduce mature dramatic poetry into Iranian culture, celebrates and manifests a distinctly Persian cultural identity through writing in a completely Arabic-free Persian language. Beyzaie's use of language in these plays is close to the equivalent of a contemporary English author using only words from before the Norman Conquest of the eleventh century, when Germanic English and Norman French blended together to become the form of English that would evolve into the language spoken today. Note, however, that Farsi has evolved less than has English over the past millennium, and so to a contemporary Farsi reader, reading Beyzaie is closer to the equivalent of reading Shakespeare than of reading Chaucer.

Beyzaie's use of antiquated language yields further literary complexity than does simply the act of echoing an ancient tongue. For though his grammar and diction are old-fashioned, Beyzaie's construction of language is, again, deceptively inventive and modern. Take, for example, the opening lines of the first play in the trilogy, *Azhdahak*, which we have translated as,

> Lo, the sleeping dragon of the night, mouth agape wider than ever and
> with a greater roar, swallowed the fully sleeping hero of the day. And the

hurricane rose with a cry of sorrow and regret. And the fully sleeping hero of the day opened his eyes, and found himself dead. And the fearsome dragon of the night crawled upon his claws, and pulled himself onto the chest of the sky.

Here, and throughout the trilogy, Beyzaie utilizes surreal, contemporary images with an almost quantum sense of postmodern motion. Characters express post-realistic feats of grandiose movement or chaotic leaps and bounds of mental anguish and dissociative identity, all reflecting, again, a strikingly contemporary dramatic battle between the individual outcast and the oppressive world. Beyzaie's blending of old and new, of ancient language and modern imagery, of the stories of yore and the conflict of the present, defines his distinct voice as an unsung master of world drama.

The great challenge of translating Beyzaie into English rests in just how specific his work is to the nature of and culture behind the Persian language. Our aim in these plays is to remain as faithful as possible to the literal meaning of Beyzaie's original text while preserving the Renaissance nature of his mixture of medieval language and contemporary ideas and images. As stated above, medieval Persian reads to a contemporary Farsi speaker roughly as Early Modern English does to a contemporary English-speaker, and rendering a text in Middle English would be both difficult to comprehend in the present day and, more importantly, cause great difficulty in remaining faithful to the original Persian text. Logically, we have resolved to translate the plays using the grammar and diction of Renaissance English. Our three major inspirations for creating a Renaissance English voice for Beyzaie (aside, of course, from the author's own Farsi work and influences) are Shakespeare, for his mastery of English Renaissance prose and verse dramatic writing, the King James translation of the Bible, one of the great literary masterpieces of its era that also echoes elements of then-antiquated medieval language, and the Richard Francis Burton translation of the *One Thousand Nights and a Night*, a work that, while Victorian, translates a medieval Middle Eastern text into an antiquated Renaissance English much in the way we strive to accomplish here.

While all three plays in the trilogy similarly embody the dramatic styles and language described above, they are all styled in a distinct manner in their dramatic structure and particular slant of mythological revisionism, and so a brief introduction to each individual work is in order. Do note that while the plays are a trilogy in a thematic sense of bearing similar styles and ideas, and while they could be performed either individually or alongside one another (much in the manner of the *Oresteia*), each play is a distinct story and the three works do not necessarily form a single literal chronological narrative. After producing the final play of the trilogy, *Testament of Bondar Bidakhsh*, Beyzaie arranged the plays in their definitive Persian form and order in a classic volume that our text has sought to preserve and adapt in translation.

Though written second, in 1959, *Azhdahak* serves as the first play in the trilogy. It is the most surreal of the three and the least rooted in a literal depiction of a particular era or location. As such, the play functions as a sort of locus of the linguistic and sociocultural notions explored throughout the trilogy. While works of *naqqali* are generally told in the third person by an objective storyteller, Beyzaie writes *Azhdahak* largely in the first person, with the performer literally playing Azhdahak and reciting a dramatic monologue (though at times the Azhdahak character does refer to himself in the third person, allowing the performer to step out of the role and take on the place of a more traditional *naqqal*).

The basis of *Azhdahak* is the story of the eponymous mythological figure who appears in wildly divergent forms in the mythology of Persia, India, Armenia, and even Mesopotamia. The wide-reaching mythological history of the character is evidenced by the number of names by which stories refer to him, including "Azhi Dahaka," "Adahak," and, perhaps most commonly in Iran, "Żaḥḥāk." Myths of the character describe him diversely as a deity, a three-headed serpent, a dragon, a hero who slew a dragon, and a king with snakes emerging from his shoulders.

While Beyzaie incorporates many elements of the varying myths of the character into his play, his primary source is Ferdowsi's account of Żaḥḥāk in the *Shahnameh*. Ferdowsi portrays Żaḥḥāk as the spoiled son of a magnanimous foreign king who is convinced by the demon Eblis to murder his father in an Oedipal act of attaining the throne. The people of Iran then invite Żaḥḥāk to overthrow the virtuous yet hubristic Jamshid and rule Iran, Jamshid having lost the will of the people. Eblis reappears as a cook who tricks Żaḥḥāk into consuming meat before kissing the king's shoulders, out of which two horrifying snakes grow and regenerate when cut. Eblis then appears as a doctor who directs Żaḥḥāk to kill two men each day to feed the snakes lest the snakes consume Żaḥḥāk's own brain. This advice yields Żaḥḥāk's long reign of terror, finally upended by Feraydun, a righteous figure who overthrows Żaḥḥāk and chains the serpent-king for eternity atop the summit of the tallest peak in Iran, Mount Damavand.

Bezyaie's adaptation radically recasts the central character, now called Azhdahak, as a tormented outcast maligned by false narratives and only now telling his own account of his life. Although it reiterates a few designated plot points from the story in the *Shahnameh*: two snakes emerging from a man's shoulders; the injustice of King Jamshid (here called Yama as in the Indian name of that figure); and the eternal chaining of the snake-man to Mount Damavand, Beyzaie's narrative is largely an original story with echoes of its mythological origin. Beyzaie's convergence of Azhdahak's ancient origins with a surreal and abstract postmodern psychological turmoil well embodies the writer's Renaissance modernity, recasting a mythological figure as a contemporary victim of unjust tyranny, at once celebrating that which is ancient and challenging the sociopolitical realities of an unjust present. And in echoing such a broad array of mythological bases for the character in a work largely free of specific references to time and place, Azhdahak becomes a universalized figure at once decidedly Persian and yet not stuck in a mode of cultural specificity, resonating with the totality of the human experience of injustice and oppression.

Arash, the second play of the trilogy, was Beyzaie's very first dramatic work, written in 1957, when he was only nineteen years of age. An English adaptation of *Arash* has previously been produced and published by Soheil Parsa, but that version was significantly abridged and altered from the original Persian.[2] This translation of *Arash* marks the first complete English version of the play (the other two plays in the trilogy have never appeared in English in any form). Of the three plays in the trilogy, *Arash* perhaps most literally represents the text of a traditional piece of *naqqali*, albeit with its own Beyzaie-esque divergences in form.

Unlike most stories told in *naqqali* performance, the basis of *Arash* does not appear in the *Shahnameh*, though the story of Arash is a foundational and ever-present force in Persian culture, venerated annually as part of the Persian summer solstice celebration of Tirgan. The traditional narrative of the myth of Arash tells that after a devastating loss in war against Iran's enemy, the mythological kingdom of Turan, the King of Turan wickedly commands that the new border of Iran be determined by the distance of an arrow shot from the top of Mount Damavand. The brave champion archer, Arash, ascends the mountain and miracuously shoots the arrow beyond human limits, saving Iran from its enemy and preserving the kingdom. The myth of Arash dates back even to the *Avesta*, the central liturgical text of Zoroastrianism, in which the deities Ahura Mazda and Mehr grant Arash's arrow the power to soar spectacularly.

Beyzaie wrote his play in response to an epic poem by the poet Siavash Kasraei, who recounted a straightforward version of the myth as a means of fostering Iranian nationalisic spirit. As usual, Beyzaie recasts the traditional champion in a revelatory light with contemporary turmoil. Beyzaie's Arash is not a champion archer, but a lowly shepherd-horseman with no skill in archery, thrust into his fate against his will while being scorned and outcast by those around him. Challenging nationalistic fervor fueled so often by the retelling of myth, Beyzaie revises the story of Arash to question the virtue of valorizing heroism only to preserve a land full of injustice, and to critique the sociocultural habit of awaiting an external messiah figure in lieu of taking charge of one's life and one's society through finding the messiah within oneself.

2. In *Stories from the Rains of Love and Death: Four Plays from Iran*, Playwrights Canada Press, 2008.

Beyzaie's *Arash* is at once the most traditionally structured and theatrically dynamic play of the trilogy. As stated above, unlike the other two plays, which are dominated by dramatic monologue, *Arash* is written as a straightforward, third-person narrative to be performed by a single narrator. It may not even appear performative on the page, reading more like a prose story than a work of drama. However, as evidenced by its subtitle, "For One, Two, or Many, Many Readers," Beyzaie intended the text to be used as a jumping-off point for a variety of approaches in performance. It could be performed by a single *naqqal*, or by two readers trading narration and performing some scenes as dramatic dialogues, or by a group of four or five actors, or even by a group of sixty performers, with its twenty-one characters, choruses, and narrative sections divided among a large company.

Beyzaie was dissatisfied with the early version of *Testament of Bondar Bidakhsh*, originally drafted in 1961, and set it aside for thirty-six years. With the significant delay in time between the completion of two of his earliest plays and *Bondar Bidakhsh*, here we have the work of a far more developed artist; the text is notably more refined and complex than that of the earlier plays. Also diverging from the earlier plays and their solo monologue form, *Testament of Bondar Bidakhsh* is a dual monologue play. Two characters speak and while they never directly interact, their swapping monologues create a quality that feels at times much like dialogue, and so *Bondar Bidakhsh* feels perhaps more nakedly dramatic than the other two works. That being said, the play is still very much rooted in *naqqali* tradition, with each speaker delivering recitational monologues, narrating his respective history and inner turmoil.

The central figure here is again an iteration of King Jamshid, now called Jam instead of Yama. The plot surrounds Jam's mythic chalice, one of the most familiar images of Persian mythology, a device much like a crystal ball, into which Jam can gaze and observe the goings-on of the entire world. The play also elaborates on Jam's mythical underground cavern, Var, discussed in *Azhdahak* and described in more detail here as a place to house a select group of the population at the expense of the masses. The eponymous second character, Bondar Bidakhsh, the creator of Jam's chalice, is an invention of Beyzaie. Bondar is inspired by a mythological character, Jamasp, the wise counselor of King Wištāsp, from *Ayādgār ī Zarērān*, a Pahlavi drama and one of the earliest surviving plays in Iranian history.

There are obvious parallels between Yama in *Azhdahak* and Jam in *Testament of Bondar Bidakhsh*: they are clearly both iterations of Jamshid, both supercilious and self-obsessed. Yet aside from differing in name, each iteration of Jamshid demonstrates differing aspects of the mythological king. *Azhdahak*'s Yama, aptly named for the mythological deity that evolved into King Jam, appears almost cosmic in scope and power, an insurmountable force who may curse Azhdahak with infinite suffering and who displays only slight overt vulnerability and insecurity. If Yama represents the cosmic side of the Jamshid figure, *Bondar Bidakhsh*'s Jam appears conversely human, grappling with doubts and hesitations, clinging desperately to what power he yields, and succumbing to madness upon his misfortune. The human Jam reflects also the play's relative realism, and certainly the psychological realism of its characters. With *Bondar Bidakhsh*, the trilogy settles from the warped, universal surreality of the first play into a refined and intimate psychodrama, still resonant with the same themes of an outcast yearning for justice amidst oppression, but through a distinct dramatic approach.

And how prescient these themes are, both on a sociopolitical level among so many individuals living through tyranny in the modern world, and, sadly, for Beyzaie on a personal level. Despite his acclaim and vital role as the pre-eminent dramatist of Iran, Bahram Beyzaie has sadly grown to embody the very outcast status that he dramatizes in these three plays. Since 2010, Beyzaie has been living in exile and serving as the Bita Daryabari Lecturer of Persian Studies at Stanford University. Like the outcasts of his work, Beyzaie has been too forthright, too honest, too outspoken of necessary truths for the ruling powers of his land to do anything but cast him away.

Yet for all that, Beyzaie's work reflects specifically on Iran and for all it works within a decidedly Persian mode of myth and language, the deeper value of his writing and of the *Naqqali Trilogy* is wholly universal. The everpresent struggle of the outcast beats through every culture and each civilization; the convergence of ancient form and contemporary idea draws universality out of cultural specificity; and the pure beauty of poetry transcends barriers of language and culture. We hope with these translations to bring the necessary beauty and power of this master artist to a yet wider audience, and we hope this audience will find Beyzaie deserving of its attention.

Azhdahak[1]

[for one reader]

LO, THE FEARSOME DRAGON OF THE NIGHT – mouth agape wider than ever and with a greater roar – swallowed the fully sleeping hero of the day. And the hurricane rose with a cry of sorrow and regret. And the fully sleeping hero of the day opened his eyes, and found himself dead. And the fearsome dragon of the night crawled upon his claws, and pulled himself onto the chest of the sky. Beforehand, likewise – I – have seen the carrion-eater sitting atop his own carrion. And he was weeping in grief for himself. I heard him cry his sky-splitting shout. Grief overwhelmed me; and then jealousy overwhelmed me. I have never cried my sky-splitting shout. I, Azhdahak, now bound to this bond, upon this mountain; the brawny, bold, behemoth mountain – Damavand![2] And I, Azhdahak, from the moment my misfortune opened mine eyes to the world, each moment I was bound to a bond – more bound than each bond – and I have never cried my sky-splitting shout. And then jealousy overwhelmed me. Then, I opened the bond of my bound mouth; and I abandoned my long-broken heart; from toe to head – I – brought out the scream of all my screams. That was when the sky split, and from its split a fire leapt out – lightning!

Beforehand – fully – upon the sleeping valleys of this empty earth, the silence was eternal. And then clouds stood up – dark with a great roar! And the darkness hidden within the valleys, spyingly gazed – [found the hero of the day sleeping] – and darkness rose from the distant valleys. And darkness held aloft his head. And darkness – black and towering – stood up; and so – like a demon – stood up on his two feet. That was when the mad dragon of the night – mouth agape wider than ever and with a greater roar – swallowed the fully sleeping hero of the day!

---

1. **Azhdahak** The central character and namesake of the play, variations of the story of Azhdahak, often alternately rendered as "Żahḥāk" or "Bever Asp," appear throughout Indo-Iranian and Armenian mythology, with roots even in the mythology of Mesopotamia. The *Avesta*, the central religious text of pre-Islamic Zoroastrian Persia, describes "Azhi Dahaka" as a three-mouthed, three-headed, six-eyed demon. Beyzaie's primary source for his work of mythological revisionism is Ferdowsi's *Shahnameh*, the eleventh-century national epic of Iran, which portrays "Żahḥāk" as a foreign-born Iranian king possessed of a demon and with two snakes emerging from his shoulders. See Introduction for more background on the mythological basis of the play.

2. **Damavand** Mount Damavand, a silent, volcanic, snow-covered peak of the Alborz Mountains in northern Iran. Damavand itself symbolizes the land of Persia in numerous myths and legends. In the *Shahnameh*, messianic King Feraydun imprisons Żahḥāk upon the mythical mountain. The phrase "bound to this bond" refers to the binding of the character upon the summit of the mountain.

Now it is me who is bound to this bond; and a tempest lifted high! And now I hear that my scream runs to the distance and twists around himself, and comes down like a whip onto the shoulder of the sleeping city. And yet the city, eternally asleep! And now the night with all his heaviness, comes down upon my shoulder.

■ Ho, night! I, the mournful, was once upon a time a man with a pure heart, who inhabited one boundary of boundaries between day and night. I had a green plain, and a vast field. Somewhere amidst my field was where night and day met each other. And in this green land of mine, each dawn, the sun, with my singing – like a red flower – would grow. And in this green vast field of mine, fieldmen lifted their songs in admiration of well-flowing clouds full of rain. My field was so, and I lived in this field. I, the slayer of the dragon – I, the proud – who decapitated the severe, three-snouted snake, and I, who flowed the stream out of closed springs.[3] That day when Yama[4] the King set foot on our land, let me forget! That day when my frontiersman father[5] offered him red wine, and Yama the drunkard who drank much wine sliced him in twain to see which was more red, the blood or the wine. And I, who told him, "May sorrow fall upon you, ye who fill our homes with sorrow," was whipped upon his order; whipped in front of the people of the village square. And when they carried me I saw that our well-built wooden house was aflame.

■ O, night! Thou art blacker than every other night. And I saw a heart blacker than thy black. And a mightily long whip. Like an open-mouthed snake. And a mouth opened toward me. And a man with a whip in his fist! It was day. And the sun, high. And the sky, short. And sorrow, dominant. And the man raised his hand. And his hand rose higher. And the man raised his hand higher. And his hand rose yet higher. And the whip, who was in his claws, drew a black scratch over the sky. And the sun, who was bright, hid her face. And the whip twisted around himself snakily. And the people gazed with fear – briskly. And the whip landed down – blood! And with his landing, a fire within a thousand veins!

3. **I, the slayer ... closed springs**   These actions, the slaying of the dragon, the decapitation of the snake, and the flowing of the stream, are an amalgamation of allusions to deeds various iterations of the Żaḥḥāk/Azhdahak figure have performed in assorted Indian, Iranian, and Armenian retellings of the myth.

4. **Yama**   In Indian mythology, Yama is the god of the dead. Yama is an alternate name of Jamshid, a mythological Iranian king, whose name is also rendered as Jam in Middle Persian and as Yima in Avestan. The Indian Yama and Iranian Yima are both sons of a solar figure. The character Jam is further expounded upon in *Testament of Bondar Bidakhsh*.

5. **My frontiersman father**   An allusion to Merdas, the father of Żaḥḥāk invented by Ferdowsi in the *Shahnameh*. Ferdowsi's Merdas was a generous king murdered by prince Żaḥḥāk out of selfish impatience to take the throne. Here, Beyzaie describes a father-son relationship oppositely mirrored to the dynamic in the *Shahnameh*.

Thus it was whip and body; and body under the whip.

Day closed his eyes; for then the heart was beating no longer within the chest of the day. And the whips landed down; on the back of a man who was pained – though not from the whips! And the people who gathered spoke to one another, "Who is this who screams with each scratch? – The wretched must cry for him!" And they were crying themselves; for they were wretched! Thus it was whip and body; and body under the whip. And the inverted sky cried upon the death of the day. And the man had a whip and a heart of iron. I watched from darkness and pain; and I saw Yama the King, who was sober. He gazed at me deeply and he was sober. Lo – he – was drunk with his sobriety. And from the shoulders of mine the reddest blood of mine spurted out. Thus it was whip and body; and body under the whip. And the sky drove a black tent over the carcass of the day. And so it was night; and the singing of the drunkard! And the eyes of the whip saw the body no longer; and the hand of the whip searched for him to no avail. Then the earth slept. And the sky had fallen asleep long before. And then, amidst the silent dormant cosmos, only I, Azhdahak, with my pain, was awake. And my heart with the most tearless eye was crying. My reddest blood was the only bright fire upon this silent plain. I looked at myself shaking terribly. I looked at myself twisting around myself snakily. From toe to head – I – saw myself in pain. And the pain in my body from toe to head was growing. And the pain was boiling within my veins. And the pain was searching for a way to erupt. Suddenly I twisted around myself; and all my corpus was twisted around itself. And I shook; and all my corpus was shaking itself. And I plunged myself into myself; and I was plunged into myself. And then from me – from the depth of mine existence – with dread and harsh anger, two snakes, roaring and crying terribly, rose; like an outpouring of fire and smoke from the mouth of the quietest mountain! And thus – like an outpouring of fire and smoke from the mouth of the quietest mountain – and thus two snakes roaringly rose; black and red; they were blood and they were pain. And I looked into myself and I burst into tears; for mine was the snake of hatred!

Then I pondered deeply. I pondered over a distant and empty realm. And my thought pulled me toward the distant realm. And I, with the mountain of my sorrows, stood up from the earth full of pain who held me on her back. And then the wind twisted toward forests; and waves broke beside; the sky roared; the clouds wept; the universe, with pain, gave birth to another day – and I went toward the distant realm.

■ And I went toward the distant realm where I could bury mine inner snakes under the dark soil. And lo, a bird, the singer of the sorrowful song of the day, had jumped from her nest, and the man whose heart was beating with sorrow carried his inmost snakes toward the open-mouthed grave of the distant realm. O, night!

What art thou guarding with the fire of thy furious clouds? That man with his load of sorrow passed the unknown paths. He passed the silent, sleeping lands, and he passed the silent, sleeping lands. He passed the entire path with his load of sorrow; and on the path he sang no song but with sorrow. He continued until he arrived at the dry, distant realm. He saw the distant realm scatter black dust away from its eyes to see the man more clearly; and he saw that the mouth of the wide-mouthed grave opened wider. The man shouted bitterly, "Ho, empty grave of terror! I am a tired, mournful one and I came to submit mine inmost snakes to thee. Now, look at me more clearly and look at thy land; will it accept my snakes?"

The empty grave of terror opened his mouth and said, "I do not want thy snakes without thee. I have never accepted any snakes without the snakes' man. No man could ever bury his inmost snakes before he buries himself."

The man shouted bitterly, "Ho, empty grave of terror! Why dost thou not accept my snakes? Why dost thou not want my snakes without me? Will my snakes remain forever on my shoulder? Dost thou send back a tired one yet more tired?" The empty grave of terror twisted around himself; from the dry land the dark storm raised, and the dark night stood. The man listened closely; and he heard no answer!

O, night! Why dost thou rumble with the rise of thy furious, black clouds? That man shouted bitterly, "A curse upon the futile traveled path!" – A thousand years afterward, a man who passed from the distant path wept with a loud shout.

The man told himself, I will go to the city close at hand; I will build a home there for myself. And he went to the city close at hand to build a home for himself. O, night! Why dost thou rumble with the rise of thy raging, black clouds? That man with his load of pain passed from the hidden and visible, futile stray paths; and passed from the hidden and visible, futile stray paths. He passed his entire path in costly pain; and on the path he sang no song but with pain. He went to arrive at the city close at hand. He saw the silent city close at hand; and he saw the grand gate of the city agape. The man shouted bitterly, "O, grand gate agape! I am a tired, mournful one and I came to this city to build a home for myself. Now, look at me more clearly and look at thy city; will it accept me with mine inner snakes?"

The grand gate agape opened his mouth and said, "In our city, the snakes are not few and people are food for one another, and snakes and people are food for the earth; and the earth is an empty and terrifying grave. And I say three times unbroken that thou art good food for the snakes of our city."

The man shouted bitterly, "Ho, grand gate agape! I did not come here to be food for the snakes of thy city. I came from a great distance away and I came here to build a home for myself. Dost thy city accept me with mine inner snakes?"

The grand gate agape congealed. From above the city close at hand, the black cloud passed, and the black night stood. The man listened closely; and he heard no answer!

O, night! What art thou saying with thy gaping, screamless mouth? That man shouted bitterly, "A curse upon the futile traveled path!" – And three thousand years afterward, the one who passed from the distant path wept with a loud shout.

■   Then I, once more with the load of my toils, continued along my path. And along mine entire long path, I lulled mine inner rebellious snakes to sleep, playing my shepherd's pipe. And there were times when I, with mine inner snakes, drifted into sleep. And I was going; along those blind, tight, futile, unavailing paths. And I was going; along the bend of those silent, sleeping paths. And I was going; through every bottleneck, across every slope, over every hillock! I passed the city of the blind and the castle of the silent. I passed through seven chambers of the fortress. I traversed all these cities. And on my path I saw all that battles all else. Each lightning against all darkness; each defeat against all dominance. Screams against quietude; and sorrows against happiness. [And I saw myself – likewise – battling with myself.] And one day, while I was passing a path, blind and tight and futile and unavailing – and while I was playing my pipe with pain – on my path – I the one who – suddenly stopped. I looked at the endless sky; at my path that became hidden in the heart of endlessness. I stood, and looked at these two; and with the ground below my foot I shook. I asked my heart, did I escape? And the cloud of sorrow was growing upon the sky. And I howled the scream of pain, "Why did I escape?" And the cloud of sorrow was raining from the sky. So I broke my shepherd's pipe with my hard hand! And so my spirit's rebellious snakes stood with a roar. I said I will return to my city where there is no justice. Then I was standing beside the tall walls of my city where there is no justice!

■   This was the city! I looked. This was the city that was chaos, full of people who were sick, and in pain. And there were people bound together like chains! And they wept, for they were the wretched ones. I saw that their faces were bloody, and they scattered away from me; and they, who were insane, cried – but there were no saviors; and I saw the escape of the people of the world, in front of the caravan of tomorrow's day; that an invisible augur was tapping intensely with howls of fear – repeatedly – on the drum of silence! And in the city, the pyretic wind was passing; through everyone who was passing. And I saw the whip who lifted higher and higher; and he landed on the back of the weary city; and again! And I heard a scream that said, "Alas, that moment!" And the walls collapsed from this scream. And a man ripped open his chest to see whether there was a heart inside – and there was and it was weeping. And one opened a vein to know whether there was blood inside – and there was and it was scarlet! No one knew me. And I knew no one. So the darkness stood. And I saw that nocturnal carrion-eater landing on the corpse of the city. I had no tear deserving of all this. And in darkness – in the dark mist of darkness – I saw that a chain was hung. And this chain told me, "Ho,

Azhdahak, whose suffering is magnificent! Look at me clearly and listen to me closely; because I am closer than thee to thyself. Go to the mad, towering fortress who rises skyward. Yama the King is there; he will tell thee what will happen." Lo, I was going to the mad, towering fortress who rises skyward. I arrived and saw my green field where the roots of every plant were dead and where a mad, towering fortress grew; and I screamed!

■   O, night! I, the wretched one, screamed loudly! Then the mad, towering fortress turned his head; he saw a man small and worthless; but for the scream he uttered. And the towering fortress was laughing madly. And Azhdahak, on top of this fortress, saw that Yama the King was laughing.

"I am Yama the King, for whom there is no death! There are soothsayers for me; my honey and wine are theirs and their prophecies are mine. They say that tomorrow there will be a freezing, tempestuous hurricane, which will sweep the earth completely of all existence! To assassinate the oppression, and dry the root of each ugliness! So I laughed and said that I will make a fortress[6] in such a steadfast way that the hurricane cannot harm it, and the foot of the deadly wind will become eroded in its height. Now I have made the best-made fortress. I have brought into this fortress women and buffoons, and the finest makers of instruments and of wine. I have adorned this fortress of mine with comely men, eloquent men, elegant nobles, and with green and red kingly stones; and I have driven sorrow to the back of the wall of this fortress. They are saying [the people of this city are saying], 'Yama the King, ye who have all ye desire, take us to your tall fortress to shelter us from the cold of death.' And I laugh and I say that death is the best master for one who has never known happiness!"

And Azhdahak rumbles insanely, "O Yama the King, have ye left no happiness for anyone?"

Yama the King laughs and says, "I am not the one who distributes happiness to the people – O thou dragon killer, Azhdahak! I am obliged to be capable, to raise my tall fortress, and to adorn it with lords from seven selected clans. Ho – I wish thou wert far away and that no one would meet thee; that they would never speak of thee and that I would not hear of thee anymore; for in this untimely glow of dark day, what is on thy shoulders? No – I will not speak to thee anymore! I see something on thy shoulders that I have never seen before; two snakes – black and red and restless! In our ancient writings, they called a man like thee demon!"[7]

6. **Fortress**   This fortress is an allusion to the mythological cavern of Var. According to the *Vendidad*, a sacred text of Zoroastrianism, Ahura Mazda informed Jamshid of a coming terrible winter, so Jam constructed Var, an underground cavern to house and protect a select group of the population, who would then repopulate the earth after the harsh winter was to pass. Var is discussed in more detail in *Testament of Bondar Bidakhsh*.

7. **Demon**   "Div" in the original Persian. In folk, religious, and literary tradition, a *div* is an evil creature whose body is similar to a human's but stout, ugly, formidable, and with horns and a tail.

Azhdahak fell into himself and twisted around himself, and with all his power, he cried his loudest roar of pain from within his bones. "I did not want to be a demon! I did not want to be a demon!" And five thousand years afterward, the one who was always passing from the distant path wept within a maniacal babel.

Lo, Azhdahak was screaming; behind the tall wall of the fortress; in the desert that was dark; on the foot of the mountain that was very high; under the weight of the clouds that were heavy; – and the fortress was silent like the sleeping mountain!

■ O, night! Thou remindest me of the sea, wherein it, as an army – [led by anger] – attacks and overpowers the sand. Thou remindest me of the black, burdensome, and brawny storm that sweeps the earth completely of all existence! I went to the mouth of the ditch where the storm was sleeping; and with my scream of fear I woke him up, and said, here I am! And then, the deadly dark wind, the deadly, difficult, striking wind that has swept away all existence, with its terrifying magnitude, was standing in front of me. Smoking fog twisted around himself and grew fully; at every instant grating the ground under my feet! So, I closed mine eyes and sang: a curse upon that moment and that place wherein my being emanated from the affection of two people to step onto the path of hatred. A curse upon that moment and that place wherein I was born into the cosmos. A curse upon that moment and that place wherein I defeated the severe three-snouted snake to bring envy to the heart of villains. And a curse upon thee, tempestuous demon wind – if I am not the first to be hunted by thine anger; for it is better for me not to witness the death of the people in this scornful manner thou holdest in thy mind; I do not tolerate seeing the suffering of any servant. Understand me that I came here on mine own foot!

So, he – the deadly, difficult, tempestuous wind – opened the bond of his mouth with that roaring thunder and told me, "Ho, Azhdahak, thou hast been born to assay the solitude alongsidest thee and to assay the suffering alongsidest thee, and the pain." He – the black, burdensome, and brawny storm – told me, "Ho, Azhdahak, thou wilt not die; thou wilt not die, Azhdahak, unless Yama the King dies first." [And I pondered.] Lo, the dawn's sky is silent. [I looked at this silence. Toward that fleeing white-feathered bird; toward this last bird] and he roared thunderously, "In this silence there is something that beats his wings" – [and it was my heart]. Then that smoke-colored infinity [in him the tempestuous roaring winds all] of such as a camel, water buffalo, boar, and skittish wolf, hastily passed two sides of me, and somehow blizzards and thunderstorms and hail came down onto the city – [upon the people to whom the door of the tall fortress was closed] – and roaring, storming, and raining were starting; ruining the homes, and peeling the earth! I saw that the almond and fig trees had forgotten their root. And a man was burying his tearlessness. I saw how the deadly rapid frozen-breath wind like eight black horses and eighty black horses and eight hundred black horses –

passage to passage – galloped toward the elusive people. And I saw too how the heart of woman was separated from husband, the fraternity of brother was cut from brother, and the covenant of friend was broken from friend. And too, how the mass wail and whine of mourners were not heard; the painful groan of a mother, petrified on her knees – for the life of her beloved – the groan froze on her face; and how the cry of an infant stayed unanswered! So, the gates of the sky closed; and the mouth of the earth opened. Hearts no longer beat, and blood was not red, and hands were opened, and eyes were closed, and tears had dried, and the deadly wind was conqueror of all. And no one sighed any longer, and no one heard any song, and no one saw any sunlight, and no one suffered, there was no chain closer to him than the chain that was himself. I wept and I saw that the memoir of paths became complex, and the limb of the fables froze. The visible aqueduct became hidden, the borders of the plain reversed. There was no affection left. And there was no bird. And a song has not sprung. And the gates of the sky were closed. And the gates of the sky closed. And the gates closed. Closed. Close!

■   It had finished. The dark and difficult and dreadful storm had finished. O, night! Thou remindest me of the storm for which there is no end!

Lo, I was pondering. Over a city that never seemed to exist. And over the people who never seemed to exist. And I saw that a nocturnal carrion-eater rose from beside the corpse of the city. And I rose. With the load of my sorrow, I rose from the earth full of pain who has held me on her back. Lo, I was face to face with Yama the King; within his closed dam! For my snakes, there were roars; their venoms were restless to poison – [I have gone to Yama the King] – and he laughed deplorably and taunted me.

"With which venom's snake wilt thou kill me? No sting would impact my snake's existence, as I am venom myself from head to toe!"

Now the roars of my snakes are silent! Thou hast never seen a snake pour his venom onto his own body and my snakes have poured their venom onto themselves; and now their roars are silent. I cried, "Ho, self-reliant Yama, then ye kill me!"

Yama the King laughed no further. Laughed no further and said, "There are soothsayers for me; their prophecies are mine. They told – they told me, the proud one – if I murder thee, I will be dead. I will not murder thee, Azhdahak. I will build a city again and then more cities. I will release people there from the classes of women and of buffoons and of soothsayers and of nobles and of apprentices. I will create other servants – frightened of the poison of my tongue, my tongue that is on my command; the steely sting of the blade! So, the rebellion will not be with them and they will fully employ my command!"

I, Azhdahak, dropped my head down with pain and I raised it with pain; I looked at him with my massive sorrow; and then all my limbs became a scream. "Ho, self-reliant Yama, I will fight with you!"

Thus it was me, the lonely one, cleaving the high pillars of the fortress with my dogged fingertips. Lo, the warrior of the day yearned to throw the javelin; though the combatant of the night raised the shield. I realized that cleaving the fortress required many hands. My hand was not many hands. The combatant of the night was roaring as I was! And none of the pillars of the tall fortress were cleaved by my fingertips. And the tall fortress was stronger than ever before!

■   Now it is me. Standing on this height. And my stare gazes. And under my foot are many cities. And in the cities, the dead are raising the best-built fortress. They look at one another in silence, and in their hearts they bid farewell. And under the scream of that whip they are silent. And the sun of the dead is dark. And Yama the King, the god of this land. And the roar of steely clouds, the only thunder of the cities of the dead. So I go ahead and I scream, "Woe be the whips for they will be broken; and woe be the tall fortresses for they will fall. I am Azhdahak, who is the child of the pain of the earth, I am the one whose scream is loud from behind the years! I am the one who has carried these black snakes on my shoulders for years. And I carry my corpse – that is rusted – from this day to that." And this is the bitter scream of the earth I am sharing with thee, "Woe be the whips for they will be broken; and woe be the tall fortresses for they will fall." The earth says, "Thou, ashamed one, stay strong upon me; the shaking of each joint of thine is shaking my spirit." She says, "Thou, back-bent one, thou art the child of the earth; take a respite before thou comest back to me in thy heart, be a crypt for death. O, man, look up, toward the sky; and see that a cloud of whips has covered the sky. I came to remind thee of the sky which is dark from whips! Justice out of this injustice; ignominy be far from thy spirit; hast thou heard the name of prosperity? Hast thine ear never been familiar with such gems: happiness and brightness and justice and compassion?"

This was my scream for which there was no answer. For I saw that eyes were open without sight and that ears were closed! O, night! For what art thou searching in this dry desert of sky? My scream passed from their faces and they were dumb-struck! So I see Yama the Lord who calls from above the fortress, "I am the Lord of this realm, and it has been many centuries since we have been dead! So I tell thee directly that I brought thee signs from the sky. The sign of salvation and the sign of retribution. These signs show that a hideous man shall appear from the base of the snakes whose food shall be your brains! On his tongue there shall be poison that is the most everlasting poison, and there shall be magic in his speech more deceptive than magic. I brought signs for you from the sky; the sign of gold pieces, and the sign of black whips! These signs say that each speech holds a dual secret, that they are like each other as two seas and they are far from each other as two seas! The bitter, portentous signs say woe on him whose screams shake the dead; for the whips are more everlasting. And woe on him whose tongue is a dragon; for I made the chains for hand and foot. This is the command of thy Lord, 'Bind him; with the tightest bond!'"

So the whips are landing; and the dead are rising. They race toward me. And before them the iron of a blacksmith, and in his fist, gold pieces![8] And the demon of night, he arrives billowing. And I close mine eye. And the night shadows over me. And I open mine eyes with pain. And I find myself in this bond in which Yama the Lord held me; upon this brawny, bold, behemoth mountain – Damavand! And I found the chain closer than myself to me.

■   Now it is me, carrying this mountain on my shoulder. And under my foot, a city. And the people are asleep. The dead, immortal, are asleep. And I am left alone with my confused cry. I remember that deadly, tempestuous wind who told me, "Ho, Azhdahak, thou wilt not die; thou wilt not die, Azhdahak, unless Yama the Lord dies first!" – And I see the night, with all his heaviness, landing on me. And I am still alive!

8. **The iron ... gold pieces**   An allusion to Persian folk hero Kaveh, the blacksmith. In the *Shahnameh*, Kaveh rebels bravely against the cruel reign of Żaḥḥāk and ultimately constructs the weapon with which Feraydun defeats the demon-king and takes rule of the kingdom. Beyzaie's brief revisionist implication that Kaveh was bribed by Jam to defeat the snake-man is deeply ironic, given that Kaveh, the blacksmith has become ingrained in Persian culture as a heroic embodiment of the virtuous common man.

Arash[1]

[for one, two, or many, many readers]

THEY, MEN, MEN OF IRAN, with their heart, with their weeping heart, saying, "What can we do now? For our bows broke, our arrows fell before their target, our arms were weak." And this was so. For they came from the long war. For the long war was toilsome. For the bowman could not be told from the bow, the archer could not be told from the arrow. And traceless men, a thousand thousand, came from distant realms. From the realm of the finest bows, and the realm of the smoothest lassos. From the realm where the four winds blow, and the plain of the flowing river. And so, every person came from every place. Of them – of those men – none ever returned to their own realm, none! And hearts full of sorrow; for the sky was black. For the sky itself was invisible. For the sun had escaped. For the moon hid herself away. For the clouds wept. But for a trace of lightning, but for a trace of lightning, there was no light upon the war, upon the men at war. And how shall a green plant rise from the ruddy earth? So, no green plant has risen from the ruddy earth. And the green trees fade into yellow, and the red flower decays into black. And each man is a storm-battered plant with dried roots.

■ And he – the horseman, Arash – wracked in thought. With wrinkled brow, he gazes out over the horizon [resembling the smile of a scoundrel]. He, a moment before, buried the bloodied corpse of a horse. Now he glares at the ruddy dust that the wind carries from the land of war. He stares with malaise out into the plain, hearing the familiar din. He knows from his father that every defeat shares the same image. In this dust of dawn, he stares at men; men, those thousand thousand, who came from the realms full of mountains and of meadows [clouds upon the mountains, flocks upon the meadows], they wonder whether they can return to their mountains, to their meadows [the tall mountains, the vast meadows], they wonder. Then, a bellowing whinny, a horse's hoof hits the ground, and the earth is filled with limbs of men, and the body of the earth is full of new wounds. And he, the horseman, Arash, kneeling upon the ground, grasps bloody dirt. In front of his eyes, battle – the battering of drum, the thundering of cymbal and timpani,

---

1. **Arash** A heroic archer in Iranian mythology. Various historical and modern texts recount the fabled story of the great archer who was tasked with shooting an arrow to determine the border of Iran after a terrible defeat in the Iranian-Turanian War. Arash is one of the most notable messianic heroes of Persian culture. See introduction for more background on the mythological basis of the play.

the roar of the masses in armor. He shuts his eyes; he sees that the sun has escaped. That the moon has hid herself away. That mountains tremble. That the plains are tight. That the sky falls down and the earth rolls up. For the rain of clouds, for the roar of wind, for the striking of lightning, Alborz[2] rises from sleep. Alborz, who knows the secret of the world, who is the true witness to the first circling of the sun. Who watches men over foothills, being born and born. And again, watches them die and die. And he – towering Alborz – with the circling of the sun and with the birth of men, he weeps and weeps. He is the only one who knows that men's lives, one, two, a thousand – are worthless, and that everything else is more worthless. And Alborz, who is the tallest of the seven skies, and Alborz – who is the tallest of the tallest – rises from sleep; and he sees the war where men – feet on the earth, head to the sky – slash their swords and slash their swords with their anger. And when the light has escaped, and when the world has darkened, and in that darkness, where white cannot be told from black and men cannot be told from men Alborz hears screams and hears screams; traceless scream of traceless man. And Alborz – the towering, who owns all secrets – he heard everything, and he remained silent. The grief of each man in the heart of Alborz was as heavy as the mountain.

■   Now through the heart of the dust, a call. Coming closer; close. And a hand wipes the dust; the Commander. He stands on one foot, the other is wooden. A sword is his cane. Four mirrors on his armor shine, but they shine red. He says, "Ho! Thou, Kashvad,[3] thou knowest archery very well. Thy bow is bent further than the back of the sky. Ho! Kashvad, one arrow, one arrow of thine – if thou releasest it – how far will it fly?" And Arash looks at Kashvad stand up. Among the dust, he sees the archer stand up like a mountain. With his torn, leather garment. Dust sits on his long hair. His white beard is disheveled. His arm is as sturdy as ten arms. Leaning on his hard bow. Arash hears that the Commander says, "Ho! Thou knowest archery well, and thine arrow bears the wings of a phoenix. Ho! Thou, Kashvad, one arrow, one arrow of thine, if thou shootest it with all thy might, how far will it travel?"

He – Kashvad – says, "One *parasang*."[4]

A cry rises out from the troops. They yell, "Kashvad! Away! Away! To the

2. **Alborz**   The modern Persian name of a mountain range in northern Iran, rendered as "Harā Bərəzaitī" in Avestan and as "Harborz" in Middle Persian. The Alborz mountain range and its highest peak, Damavand, play a prominent role in the historical texts of Tabaristan and in Iranian legend.

3. **Kashvad**   A fabled Iranian warrior and the ancestor of the Gōdarziān family. In the *Shahnameh*, he is mentioned as bearing a golden helmet and as being the father of the hero Gōdarz.

4. **Parasang**   A historical Iranian unit of walking distance of ambiguous length, its closest European equivalent being the league. The unit has evolved into the modern *farsang*, a metric unit of six kilometers.

Turanians![5] They who appear as demons! And tell them thou wilt release the arrow! And wheresoever thine arrow lands, Kashvad, that shall be Iran! Wheresoever thine arrow lands!"

The Commander says, "Now, thine orders!"

Kashvad screams, "I will not obey!"

So the Commander, through the heart of the dust, looks at Kashvad, red-faced. "Kashvad ... the wind is blowing and I did not hear thee."

Kashvad says, but calmly, "No one man is defeated in war; we are all defeated. If I release this arrow, I will be cursed forever. Tomorrow, those who remain captive, troop after troop, will say it was Kashvad's arrow that gave us to the enemy."

Then the Commander on one foot yells, "We have sacrificed a hundred men for each parcel of land we lost. Now thine arrow will move one *parasang* farther."

Kashvad looks over the plain, magnificently. "One *parasang* is worthless; now a country is lost."

Then the Commander moves closer with his engorged face, "When there is no remedy, this could be a hope, Kashvad. Hope for a parcel of freedom."

Kashvad asks, "Freedom?"

And the Commander answers, "From slavery."

Then Kashvad howls, "Before this enemy came, there was no slavery?"

The Commander, speechless, gazes out over the wind. Through the dust five guards approach.

Kashvad throws his head down, "They have not defeated us. We were defeated before this."

And then, Arash, the horseman, stares at the dark sun that had risen from behind that height, that mountain. Among the dust, shadows – afar – crawl; the living and the dead together. From the marsh, a bird is singing. And now the Commander, like a shadow, starts to speak. "Of whom art thou speaking? The people thou worriest over are not with thee. What makes thee think these people thou carest for have any compassion for thee? Thou art like the wheel of a chariot that has become stuck in the mud. Look, Champion, how they will burn the chariot even while it breaks under their burden. I did not want this war. Myself, I am merely a plaything of this war. That time when everyone should have been united, we were divided; every man thought only of himself. Everyone went his own way. Many famed champions were abandoned. Many lone heroes fell prostrate. Where are the valorous? Yea, this oppression is ours and we are all oppressors. Defeat was all that united us. Now each voice throughout the land is

---

5. **Turanians** People of the land of Turan, a historical region in Central Asia. In Middle Persian and Islamic sources, their mythological descent is traced to Tūr, one of the sons of Feraydun. Disputes resulting from land allocated by Feraydun to his sons Tūr and Iraj led to the fabled Iranian-Turanian wars that serve as the backdrop of this play.

crying for liberation from the enemy. There is no more place for hesitation. Mine ear is closed to any excuse. And I am asking thee, Kashvad, with all thy wisdom, to gather all thy bravery. This is thee and this is the covenant."

And Kashvad gazes into the wind. "With this arrow, nothing will change."

The Commander cries, "Dost thou not see that the enemy has created a jungle of spears, that they are more impatient than the restless sea, impatient to create an image more terrifying than their last? The enemy can destroy us."

And Kashvad yells, "They destroyed us with a laugh. What can an arrow do? What is the purpose of this covenant? They, the derelicts, know our arrow will not travel far."

Then the Commander moans, "The enemy is stubborn and we cannot overcome them."

And Kashvad says, to the wind, "To the old frontier, the liberation of the people depends upon this arrow."

The Commander's face fills with rage; he is furious. "It is no longer in our hands to set them free."

Now Kashvad, with anger, says, "But who set them into bondage?"

And now the lance of light strikes a thousand pieces of earth, and a bird wails; here and there people fall to the ground. Among this wailing, an old man starts to moan, following him, the remaining men of several tribes and peoples, "How swift is our fate before the dusk! What is left of our manhood? We are a laughing stock in the face of the cosmos. Was not the dark grave of death more deserving for us?"

Then suddenly, the Commander roars, screams, rises, and cries out, "Ho! Man! Brave Champion, rise! This is a covenant upon which we agreed!"

And then Kashvad, staring into the Commander's eyes, says, "I did not make this covenant." [Kashvad breaks his bow and throws it to the ground.]

The Commander is aghast. "This is an order from the highest command."

Kashvad says, "In defeat, no man is higher than another."

Then that Commander, with dagger in hand, shouts, "Kashvad, think of others!"

And Kashvad fumes, "Who said I am not thinking of others? This is a covenant between masters regarding the lives of their servants. This arrow will only determine which slave belongs to which master. Now troop after troop waits. But whoever commands me to shoot the arrow cares not for the people, he is tired and wants only the war to end. But I do not know myself apart from the people. If I cannot free them, I will stay with them."

He said that and it was magnificent!

The Commander, dumbstruck, cries out to the wind, "Tomorrow they will trample us."

Kashvad has already left. "I will submit to the hooves of the horses, but not to this abuse."

And then he goes away. Through the heart of red dust, he goes away. And Arash sees five corporals approaching the Commander. The eyes of the horseman stare through the dust. He searches for Kashvad. He runs to him. He calls his name. Kashvad stops. He takes his hand and brushes away the dust to find the source of the sound. But he sees nothing [he thinks it must have been the wind] and he carries onward to a burnt tree. Now Kashvad stands beside a tower with a horse shattered by an arrow, and Arash reaches him.

Arash says, "Champion!"

Kashvad stops to look at him and says, "My name is Kashvad."

Arash says, "May thy name become immortal! I have been at thy side."

Kashvad answers, "I have never seen thee before."

The horseman says, "I was a shepherd in this land and now I am a horseman to the troops."

Kashvad retorts, "What art thou doing in my way, horseman?" And Arash, with all his passion, says, "I admire thee, Kashvad."

Suddenly, the man's whole body shivers, he looks at Arash, the torment in his throat halting his speech. He hardly says, "Get away from me."

Arash turns down his head in shame and Kashvad vanishes. And through the dust Arash hears someone call his name. A sentry appears.

"Arash, they are looking for a messenger to go to the enemy. I told them that thou knowest their language well and that thou wilt deliver the message intact. Now turn and look there."

Then Arash turns his head and sees the Commander drawing him over with his finger.

"Thou art a good horseman, Arash, but a poor soldier. Now there are no horses left to tend; thou must be our envoy to the enemy. Go to them and tell them that one day is very short, and that one respite until the sun sleeps is not sufficient for us. We need more time beyond the next sundown."

And Arash gazes into the distance. And across the fog he sees a troop of enemy soldiers, smiles on their faces, bowls of wine in their hands. Flags raised, lances at their sides.

■ Now, land. Dark land. Once upon a time our homes rose on this dark land.

■ Then Arash blows the *nafir*.⁶ The king of Turan⁷ looks at Arash, his eyes red as the sun. He laughs at Arash and says, "Was there not a single horse left of thy troop?"

---

6. **Nafir** An ancient Iranian trumptet made from the horn of an animal.

7. **King of Turan** Though Beyzaie leaves this king of Turan unnamed, he clearly represents Afrāsīāb. The most prominent of the Turanian kings, Afrāsīāb is depicted in the *Shahnameh* as a force of evil with magical powers bent on destroying Iranian land.

Arash turns around, looking at the land, and says, "My horse was grazing."

And the king replies, "Which pasture did not burn? [moving closer to Arash] Art thou the archer?"

And then Arash responds to the king in Turanian, "I am the horseman of the troops and I bear a message from our army with this token of red ruby."

The king asks, "What happened to thy previous messenger? He was injured."

Arash answers, "He drew his last breath."

The king replies, "Every man shall draw his last breath unless he submits. Now deliver thy message. Thou hast mine ear."

Arash says, "One day of respite is not enough for us."

"Not enough?"

"Our archer is tired."

The king looks up at him, "Archer? Is that not thee?"

Arash says, "I am a horseman."

The king howls, "But I heard thee say it was thee."

Arash shakes. "I did not."

The king shouts at him, "Who is this man who calls me a liar?"

And Arash does not respond.

The king of Turan says calmly [with great fire in his eyes], "What was thy name?"

"Arash."

"And thou art the archer."

Arash takes a step back. "Nay. I have never been a good archer."

The king says, "This is excellent! Thou wilt shoot the arrow!"

Arash cannot believe his ears. "The wind is blowing and I did not hear your words."

The king of Turan laughs. "Thou didst hear, Arash. Thou wilt uphold this covenant."

Then Arash, with suspicion, looks at the king's smile, and timorously says, "I am a worthless man. It is not kingly to humiliate a worthless man."

The king of Turan bellows, "Dost thou advise me?"

[And seven corporals unsheathe their swords.]

Then, calmly, the king says, "Thy masters accepted this humiliation."

Arash turns his face. "Never."

Kicking the ground, the king says, "I brought thy people to their knees, they asked for my reconciliation and I granted that. They sought peace, and I approved. I offered a covenant by which they could determine their border with an arrow and they accepted out of fear of my wrath. They swore strong oaths to uphold this."

Arash laments to the wind, "We have been devastated."

And the king laughs, "And will be more devastated when thou, the one I choose, releasest the arrow."

Arash turns away his face. "Not me!"

And then the king laughs again. "Yea, Arash, thee. We reached an agreement but we never named the archer. Now I have named him, and by the gods I will remain true to my word." Arash blushes, "You try in vain. They will never accept this."

And then he – the angry king – he looks at his army. Ready in their armor. Their ebony banner shaking in the wind. They open their mouths to laugh.

Arash, stunned, says, "This is humiliation."

And then, the king of Turan smiles bitterly. "Once upon a time they humiliated us. Let it be our day now. Thou art the final arrow in my quiver. Know that I could cut all of you down with my sword."

And Arash asks, "Why have you not?"

The king stops laughing. "Nay, Arash. They should stay and tell their children what they saw us do."

Then the king shouts, "Wine." [Wine-bearers approach.]

Arash says, "I am not thirsty."

The king changes his face – A moment of pause – He says, coldly, "I had compassion for thee."

Arash, again, rages, "I am not thirsty."

The king of Turan looks at him, blood rushing to his face, shaking with anger. "Arash, thou hast not yet told me what happened to thy previous messenger."

Arash screams, "He died!"

The king says, "He was more fortunate than thee. I will destroy thee a hundred times."

Then he goes away. And Arash hears the king call a name. This name is familiar to Arash. He sees a shadow emerge from the back of the back of the red king's chamber. Seeing him, a tremor rushes through Arash's body. Arash raises his ear and hears, "Ho! Hoomann,[8] what dost thou know of Arash?"

And a man – with the strength of ten men – "I have never heard that name."

The king says, "The owner of this name is now here. Look at him carefully and tell me what sort of archer he is."

Then Hoomann turns his head. He searches with his eyes, the sight is completely unfamiliar. He sees a paltry man. He is the sole footman among men on horseback. Hoomann says, "I have never seen this man among the warriors."

The king: "Swear it."

---

8. **Hoomann**   Radically reimagined here as a traitorous hero of Iran, Hoomann is a celebrated Turanian warrior in the *Shahnameh*.

He: "Upon my life."

Then the king laughs and shouts, "We must write a letter. Ho! Hoomann, be ready; a letter in Parsi."[9] The king goes away toward a purple wall and stops at the door. "He was one of you but now he is one of us."

Arash knows that his knee is shaking and that his vision is becoming blurred. In agony, he opens his eyes and finds himself in front of Hoomann. "Thou, Champion, slayer of demons, we thought thou wert dead."

Hoomann does not look at him.

Arash screams, "Why hast thou betrayed us?"

And Hoomann, startled by Arash's scream, says, "There, I was the mule of my tribe."

Arash says, "Thou art no mule here?"

Hoomann says, "I have escaped from injustice to injustice, from tyranny to the enemy. But what dost thou know of a warrior's life? Since I must submit, I will do so to the one who feeds me better."

Arash says through his teeth, "But Champion, thou foughtest against the enemy!"

And Hoomann looks off into the distance, at the dust. "I wanted to know if there was still love for my land inside me, and there was none!"

Arash, stupefied, says, "This is horrendous."

Then, insane laughter. They see that out from the purple wall the Turanian king returns; the crown on his head, a red garment over his shoulder, a bowl of wine in his hand, and the king's jewel on his finger. He laughs. "Now we must write a kingly letter. Look up to the sky, Hoomann. The carrier pigeon is eager to fly."

Arash says, "I will return."

And the king laughs again. "Go, Arash. Faster. When thou arrivest thou wilt find that thy friends are no longer thy friends."

Now Arash is far away. He thinks about these words and he does not know what to make of them.

■ The sun shines. He turns his face upward. A white pigeon flies like the wind. Now Arash walks through burned canebrake. He speaks to his heart. "I was a shepherd leading the sheep. When my heart desired, I sang for the sheep. When it did not, I slept beside the sheep. Why did I come here? – Why was my sleep broken by this clamor? Why did this wind scatter my flock of sheep?"

He goes, and he drinks no water from the bloody lagoon. The tall levee beckons him to stay but he goes. He looks along his way, and amid the red dust he sees a wooden tower still standing. Suddenly, a great wave of thunder rips through the

---

9. **Parsi**   An alternative name for the Persian language.

dust. He turns his eyes and sees the Commander coming forward from the tower. The Commander's mouth is agape with screaming. He carries something in his hand, Arash does not know what it is. Then Arash stops and sees the Commander standing in front of him; the Commander, with his flaming sword in his hand, with all of his anger, screams at him, "Is this true?"

And Arash knows nothing.

That Commander, with drawn sword, shouts louder, "Be honest with me. Art thou with them?"

And Arash does not believe what he hears.

Then that furious Commander, shaking with anger, shouts, "This is the carrier pigeon that sat on our tower and this is a message with the seal of the enemy!"

And Arash, speechless, still has no answer.

The Commander knocks his sword to the ground. He twists around himself in lunacy with screams like rubble. "O! I acted foolishly! I heard that thou wert in their region before we were, but I did not smell thy malice. I knew that thou spokest their language but I did not think to doubt thee. [with pain] I gave thee my token. I trusted thee, Arash. Why hast thou deceived us?"

And Arash screams, "I have not!"

Now the Commander crushes Arash with his eyes. "There is no more place for lying. This is a message from the enemy with a rigid oath to the Gods of Sand. They will submit only to the arrow that thou shootest."

And Arash kneels down on the ground.

The Commander still cries out, "Thou, who art the weakest archer, whose arrow will fly no further than his arm!"

Arash has no answer. He looks around feebly and sees five corporals emerging from the dust. Their eyes are on the Commander and now the Commander speaks, "Yea."

Arash screams, "Nay."

And the Commander takes his sword. "Yea, Arash, thou hast submitted to them, thou sworest an oath to them. And this is a message written in Parsi. This may even be written by thee."

The horseman says, "I do not know how to write."

And the Commander: "I do not believe a single word from thee anymore. This was written by thy hand. And thou knowest that very well."

Arash says, "I do not know anything. I do not know."

Then the Commander hesitates, calmly, holds back his sword, and says, "I heard that thou admiredst Kashvad when he refused to shoot the arrow. Why?"

Arash is silent.

The Commander shouts, "Why?"

And Arash answers strongly, "Do ye think I am a traitor?"

"I have no doubt."

"Then kill me."

The Commander shouts, "So, I will."

Arash sees the sharp sword lift to the sky and he closes his eyes upon the blazing of the sun. Now he hears a scream in the wind. He opens his eyes and sees one of the corporals shielding him from the sword. The corporal says to the Commander, "Sheath your sword! If ye touch but one hair of this dog, that lunatic king will make a flood of blood!"

Then the Commander, sword in hand, is frozen like a stone. He begins to moan, deplorably. He throws his sword on the ground. "Thou knewest this too, Arash. This is his message."

While they are speaking, a sentry arrives and throws a bow onto the ground. "This is a present from the king of Turan to Arash."

Arash does not understand anything but he hears that the Commander says, "Arash, dost thou still deny it?"

Amidst his hesitation, Arash hears laughter through the dust. Of the corporals, one is older than the rest. He steps forward and says, "This belonged to Hoomann."

All of the corporals kneel at once. The Commander looks toward the dust and speaks sadly, "Let us remember that Hoomann never made an oath with the enemy. His was an honorable death as he left no trace of himself. When he was left alone in front of the enemy masses, he was unafraid and he shred their bodies like autumn leaves. They rode over him in their horses so that his great body was torn asunder beneath the hooves to become one with the earth."

The corporals cry softly. "His possessions were all in the hands of the enemy. We looked and looked but could not find them. Arash, horseman, we wish thou wert more like Hoomann."

Then the Commander goes away, and the others follow. Arash sees that he is alone, and his bones ache.

■   The beating of timpani, and the call of the *nafir*. There – close to the wooden tower – corporals consult with the Commander.

"Now sentries of the five towers wait for the archer."

"Never!"

"That insane man only accepts the arrow that this dog shoots!"

"Let us not start the war again, Commander!"

"Even if this creature's arrow flies no further than his arm?"

"It does not matter how far the arrow flies. Without this archer, we will have another bloodbath."

"Alas, why did I not kill him?"

"It is not too late, Master, he will return."

"What?"

"We are tired of this war."

Then they see through the dust a group of soldiers walking toward Arash; sneakily, with stones in their fists. This is the beginning of the stoning, and they gallop with drawn swords to scream at Arash.

■   What cloud is in front of the sun? The sentry becomes a shadow between the sun and Arash. "Arash, take this arrow."

And Arash hears nothing but the wind.

He stands in front of Arash, tall, and Arash still lies on the ground.

"Stand up, Arash."

And Arash raises his head, and with his dead eyes, it seems Arash is not himself. Arash looks at him and says, "Wast thou here when they smote me like a worm?"

"Yea."

Arash moans, "I have not told them that Hoomann is still alive."

And he, in the dust: "There is no need. Everyone knows that."

Then Arash shakes with all his body. "They know that?"

"Yea. Hoomann is still alive. He is alive in our hearts."

And Arash falls to the ground again. "What dost thou want from me?"

"Thou knowest well, Arash."

Arash shouts, "I will never shoot the arrow."

"Yea, thou wilt, Arash, thou wilt refuse it a few times but thou wilt ultimately shoot the arrow."

Arash says, "Who said that?"

"Is this not so?"

Arash says through his teeth, "I will not shoot the arrow!"

And the sentry, amidst the dust and light, whispers to Arash softly, "If thou dost not release it, our master – that grand master – will send thee back to thy friends, hand-tied, upside-down, hanging from a mule, thy body slashed with whips, and he will tell them it was Arash who broke the covenant. It was him. [He looks at Arash maliciously.] Will thy friends forgive thee for this?"

Arash closes his eyes. "I have no friends. I am not on their side."

Arash hears a laugh like poison. The sentry says, "Is that so?"

And Arash cries, "Thou wilt not believe me either?"

And now the sentry gives no reply.

Arash twists himself in disgust. "I cannot look in the eyes of mine own people anymore. I cannot. Alas, why did he not kill me?"

The sentry stands without moving.

Arash says, "What should I do? What compensation can there be? I will knock my ten fingers on stone. My feet that brought me through the enemy. My claw, who wants to take the bow and arrow. What should I do? What can I do to convince a single person of the truth?

His gaze upon Alborz. "I do not know any way."

And now, in Arash's mind, an arrow flies like the wind.

The sentry says, "I will return to my master. What shall I tell him?"

Arash stands on his feet and roars to Alborz, "I will shoot the arrow!"

■   Now they beat the drums. They scream through horns. They make a great fire on the embankment. They release a *shahbaz*;[10] flaming javelins hanging from his tail. The sentries look from the tower; they see fire from the distant chamber with flames shooting up into the sky. They sing into the *nafir*. Now, men, men of Iran, with their scream, with their loudest scream, shouting, "Arash! Away! Away! To the Turanians! They who appear as demons! And tell them thou wilt release the arrow! And wheresoever thine arrow lands, that shall be Iran! Wheresoever thine arrow lands, Arash!" And he, Arash, he sallies forth, to the Turanians, they who appear as demons, and he shouts, "I will shoot the arrow, and wheresoever mine arrow lands, that shall be Iran! Wheresoever mine arrow lands!" And they, the Turanians, who appear as demons, they say, "Arash! Arash! Shoot the arrow! And wheresoever thine arrow lands, that shall be Iran! Wheresoever thine arrow lands, Arash!" Each Turanian speaks the speech, and for each mouth there is another word, "How far can his arrow fly? How far can his arrow fly?" And to the other side of the universe, the Turanians give an ugly smile.

■   And he, Arash, the man who has received an ugly smile from across the universe, says with his heavy heart, "How far can mine arrow fly? How far can mine arrow fly?"

■   Now a way, bent among foothills. He, on the path, his bow beside him. He looks at the horses' hoof prints on the ground and sees silent ditches. He passes a hand out of the dust. And he sees a spur thrust into the ground, erect, a plant growing upon it. And he, Arash, he sees all of this, and he passes. And when he turns his head to look at the sun, he is aghast.

■   The king of Turan sees fire from the enemy with flames shooting up into the sky, with the voice of flutes from the river; he laughs terribly, red, dark like smoke. He, with his many men, masses upon masses. A thousand flags in the wind.

---

10. **Shahbaz**   A species of goshawk, a bird of prey larger and less predatory than a hawk, also itself called a "giant hawk." This bird lives on the slopes of the Alborz, Zagros, and Caucasus mountains.

The king looks at the sun, his chalice upon his lips; the wine is bitter, his vision is blurred. Suddenly, a thought; he jolts upright and searches the chamber; his body is entirely red, and his scream is like death. "Where is Hoomann?"

The Champion comes to him. "Here."

The king looks at him. "Thy friends agreed that Arash shall shoot the arrow."

Hoomann says, "Yea. Fortune smiles upon you."

The king yells, "They have agreed, Hoomann. Is it not strange?"

Hoomann steps back. "Why strange?"

The king shouts at him, "Thou swearest he knows not of archery?"

"Yea, I swear."

"Hoomann, how, then, is Arash going to keep this covenant?"

And Hoomann is speechless.

The king shouts at him, "Hast thou lied to me?"

And Hoomann shouts, "Never!"

The king throws his wine to the ground slowly and the spear-carriers approach Hoomann.

"Hoomann, it has not been long since I have seen thee. Art thou truly with us?"

Hoomann says, "Am I not?"

The king laughs drunkenly. "Suddenly, a thought came to my mind. Perhaps thou wert with them and thou deceivedst me."

Hoomann – happy – says, "What deception! King, you will see that his arrow shall fly no further than his arm."

The curmudgeonly king says, "How confident art thou in this?"

Hoomann says forcefully, "I would wager my life on it."

Then the king looks again at the fire, and says terribly, "If thou hast deceived me, I will command men to run horses over thy body until it is one with the earth."

Hoomann looks to the sun. "It shall be so."

■   What is this narrow path that the corpse of a lone man stays in vain? He, from toe to head, boiling; on his face there is dew. He goes, his bow arched and his arrow straight beside him. A while ago he removed his heavy garments and walked far away from them. Now he hears a call. On his path up he stops and observes. From behind a cliff, a sturdy man appears. Arash sharpens his eyes, hesitates, then continues onward. And it is Kashvad that closes onto him. "Stay, Arash!"

"Thou hast heard it too, Champion?"

"Yea."

"Wilt thou be kind to me?"

"I came here to turn thee back."

Arash turns his face, and in his eyes there are a thousand questions for Kashvad.

Kashvad says, "Thine enemy has passed a thousand thousand, and thou art on thy way to make one of them free. This is worthless."

And Arash looks at the path, but he cannot take one step without a man standing in front of him like a mountain. "Tomorrow they will return to their homes, Arash, and thou wilt be alone with thy solitary heart. Thou wilt humiliate the mountain of submission of masters. This arrow is perhaps an excuse to bestow upon them plains and with those plains give them a mass of slaves."

Arash says, "Go away from my path."

And the shadow of the sturdy Champion: "Man, think of the people."

Arash screams, "I am one of them, myself."

Kashvad screams, "Does this arrow end slavery?"

Arash continues, and the man like death closes his path and says, "Nay, this is not for their benefit."

Arash shouts, "What dost thou know of benefit and harm?"

And Kashvad says, "With this arrow, there is one thing that will not change, and that is the days of the people: the people will still be servants after all. Arash, think of the slaves!"

And Arash screams, "It is not an option for me to think about it!"

Kashvad howls, "Think of the hostages."

Arash hardens like a stone. "Who is thinking of me? There is no way for me to return, Champion. I am a man of honesty and piety, and thou didst not want to hear my word. You all call me a man of lies and deceit, and I will stay that way."

And Kashvad, with his aching heart, says, "Arash, I did not believe their ugly words. But now I see that indeed thou art nothing but an enemy."

Arash capitulates, "Say that, Champion. Everyone says that. Only thou wert left! Thou hast just made a wound; leave me alone now to suffer it."

Now Kashvad, his fist is knocking on stone: "Do not come closer. I will kill thee!"

So Arash takes a step back, puts the arrow into his bow. Kashvad bellows, and Arash raises the bow above his head to shake in anger. "Great man, Champion, I have shed no blood, but now I am without fear. For me, there is no way except to go on."

Kashvad says, "Thou wilt not kill me, Arash."

Arash howls like a predator, "Yea, Champion. I know no other way."

Kashvad looks at Arash's shaking hand. "Arash, thou art not a good archer. Why wilt thou shoot the arrow?"

Arash, cries selflessly, "With the hope to die!"

Now, silence. Then Kashvad moves the mountain that is his body out of Arash's way.

■ Now he – Arash – stands in front of Arash. He is looking at him, and they both begin to walk. No one's steps are taller than the other's, and the wind blows through their hair alike.

"Do not come with me, Arash. Stay further away from me. Thou stainest me with myself."

"Where can I stay, Arash? I am the only one thou hast. Where canst thou escape from me? At dawn, I saw a black omen in the sky looking to land on someone's head and I understood that he was searching for thee."

"I did not deserve it."

"Thou deservest the worst, Arash. They scold thee for thy honesty and thou deservest it. Why didst thou not escape from the battle plain to the mountain? Why didst thou not surrender thyself to a dagger during the chaos? Why didst thou not submit thyself to the enemy as a slave? Why didst thou not bend thy back in front of the narrow-eyed people? Thou deservest it, Arash."

"I am an ignorant person. Do not torture me with wisdom. I am very far from home. Alas! I am not sure if there is any home."

"Now the world chooses thee to mock. Fear the time thine arrow will return to thee. There is no place for thee at which even a fool will not point at thee in scorn. The universe will be full of thy scream, thy scream from the blame of old women and from the moans of widows. From the sneer of a migrant and of a civilian, and from the sigh of those who grow old under the spinning wheel."

"Silence! Say no more, Arash. Do not make me the target of turmoil. Leave me alone so that thou art not burnt by my fire. And what is this that is turning through my head? What is this that runs through mine arms? What is this that races through my chest? What is this that boils in my veins? What is this power inside me? What is this power?"

"Think, Arash. Is it not hopelessness?"

"A thousand salutations to that, a thousand thousand salutations to that; even if mine arrow falls short, the arrow that is the shame of all men, and even if the universe mocks me, I will not be more disgraced than I am now."

■ Alborz – the towering, hidden among clouds – brushes the clouds aside. On his feet – he sees Arash. "Who is this approaching me with a long bow and with an arrow adorned with the feather of a phoenix? His eyes full of woe and his steps that fear nothing?" Alborz says this and Arash walks like this. There are no words on his lips, but his head is full of thoughts. "Man, thou hast been destroyed. Canst thou ever return? [Then Arash looks up.] Why didst thou come to this battle? [And the scream of Alborz comes down onto Arash ten times.] Here was a plain of demure gazelles, but now see that behind every stack of thorns, quilled hedgehogs burrow."

Then a dry gulley, and Arash passes. "A spring remembers thee with a girl at thy side; a raised eyebrow, flowing hair, full of chastity. Remember how that spring became stone and those eyes were closed. There is no foundation left from the wall and no thorn left from the garden." Arash climbs over Alborz. The ground moans beneath his feet.

■   There – from the heart of the dust – commanders pass by, their troops following, their murmurs lost in the dust. Yonder, beside the tower, timber burns, a fire guard[11] comes hastily from the smoke. He throws himself onto the ground. "Commander, I heard some horrendous words."

The Commander pivots toward him; his face is wet. "Speak."

The fire guard, timber in his hand, says, "I am not a tale-bearer, but great man, this is not justice. Our men have sworn that when Arash returns they will attack him to tear him apart joint from joint."

Under the Commander's breath, "I will not stop them."

The fire guard stops frozen. "Did I hear what you said? Have we forgotten the enemy so we can tear ourselves to pieces?"

Then the Commander bellows, "Is this not a punishment for treason?"

The fire guard is scared. "Undoubtedly. But that scoundrel will draw a sea of blood."

The Commander, looking at the third tower in the sun: "He is behind Arash until the arrow is released, but when he receives what he wants he will forget who Arash was."

■   Now, from the dust on the highland, Arash sees a shadow who stands in his way; like a stain in front of the sun. Magnificent. He is sturdy with the vigor of ten men. His javelin in his hand; his javelin straight and steely. And Arash screams, "Father, why didst thou not teach me how to cry?"

And the shadow tumbles. "I am the one who should cry. I am the one."

Arash stands in his pain. "Oh, father, have you heard it too?"

And the shadow is silent.

Then Arash, kneeling on the ground: "Do you not know your son anymore? [and then aghast] It is no wonder as I do not know myself anymore."

Now the dust vanishes and the shadow says, "Everyone has turned their back on thee, Arash. Thou art alone."

Arash screams, "I am full of hate."

"For thine enemy?"

11. **Fire guard** This character is a Zoroastrian religious worker. In Zoroastrianism, fire is a holy representation of goodness and purity. The fire guard's role is to ensure that the fire remains pure and is never extinguished.

He screams, "More for friends."

Then the shadow leans in. "Arash, is that a lie?"

A knot in the throat prevents Arash from speaking.

Now that javelin, sharp, raised. "Is that a lie?"

Arash says, desperately, "How can I convince you?"

The shadow's cry is like thunder. "I am not the one who should believe thee; look down to the plain, to the mist, to all those people who are standing side-by-side. [And then he thinks, sadly.] No one will be with thee but thyself, Arash. This arrow, release it with thy spirit if thou canst, not with thine arm."

The shadow stands magnificently, like a stain in front of the sun. Now a bird flies like the wind, and the wind is not himself.

Arash looks at his bow, calmly. "Is this not in vain?"

And the shadow says, "In vain?"

Arash says amidst the wind, "The Turanian encampments are so far away."

The shadow says, "Throw it farther."

Arash says, "As far as the meadow that was our home?"

The shadow roars, "Farther!"

Arash screams, "From here to the frontier, the people rely on this arrow."

The shadow roars, "Farther!"

Arash asks, "To the frontier?"

Now the shadow is a scream, "Farther!"

And Arash falls to the ground. "Father, teach me compassion."

The shadow: "Nay!"

Arash: "Give me strength."

The shadow: "Nay! If thou art full of hate, if thou hatest this, then I have nothing to give thee, because thou art more capable than I am. Ho! It is thy spirit that will release the arrow, not thine arm!"

He says so. And it is the most glorious speech of all.

So, Arash continues his way. He goes away. He goes farther.

■ A crevice in the mountain. There are several sentries inside; spears in their arms and daggers in their fists. A few rocks on one side, and inside of them, a fire. A soldier of Turan with a bird in his hand laughs cruelly. "Arash, if thou wert there, tell us who thou wert shouting at in the heart of the mountain. We looked sharply but no one was there except thee."

Arash stops and hesitatingly says, "Was not one there?"

The man laughs. "We did not find out. His cry was far away. His cry echoed. Like the last cry of a wounded man; very muffled. We thought it was thee."

And Arash continues his way up.

Now the sentry of Turan releases the bird, a message tied to its tail. Then a distinctively rude smile, and Arash hears from fire and glass a person speaking his own language, saying, "Art thou the one who is a friend to the enemy? That nimble one?"

From a wooden trench, some whispers. "Silence, he does not know that we know."

One answers quickly, "Why does he not know? This is a mountain and here the voice echoes."

And Arash says nothing and he continues along his way. He passes the tight bottleneck and sees the wooden trench becoming smaller and smaller every moment. Now a shield descends. Behind it, a man, feeble, shouts, "Arash, take a look at us, we are the last men thou wilt ever see. We are the sentries of the fifth tower. On thy way back, tell us how thou releasedest thine arrow on top of the impetuous summit."

Men shout but Arash goes away; higher, and he does not hear the shouting well. He sees the battle plain that is disappearing little by little, and the tower of the sentries becomes invisible bit by bit. He finds that he is hearing nothing more than the sound of his footsteps on the shoulder of the earth. And again he climbs and the seven furnaces of his body burn. He knows from his father that when a scorpion is trapped in a fire it stings itself to become ash. And he, Arash, looking at himself, sees that he is trapped in the fire of his own thoughts.

■   Then he stops; the smell of grass and dew brings him to his senses. He sees that he is trapped in the mist for a great while. Then he takes his bow with two hands, his ear alert. For he sees nothing; a harsh noise of steps; he looks back sharply. Now a man approaches, through the green, strong like a tree. Winter snow has fallen on him. He comes, straight, with flames in his eyes, his limbs trembling with warmth. He looks at Arash, deep, staring, looking at him compassionately, and the fire of his word bellows out. "Arash, do not be their hope."

Arash does not look at him, but he recognizes Kashvad. "Man, I do not know thee. But know that my heart is now tight in my chest."

The man whose words are more winning than the warrior's axe: "Arash, this freedom is not eternal. Every covenant is broken one day. Where wilt thou be that day? [And he – Arash – lips closed.] Arash, there are many obstacles ahead. If thou savest them, thou wilt be their hope and this is horrific. The hope that for every crucible a man is coming and will diminish their sorrow. And in every crisis they turn their eyes to see who is the chosen one and then they sit on their hands."

Arash cries out, "Thy word in this breeze looks like an axe that hits the roots."

The man says, "Thine arrow will release them once and enslave them forever."

Arash becomes agitated and listens. "Thou dost not spread seeds that could flourish everywhere. Thou wilt flourish thyself, like a tree that will die in winter and grow again in the spring."

Arash, with all his sorrows, turns himself to the other side; to that coarse mountain. And sees him still standing there looking forward. Then Arash looks at the man but cannot see him anymore.

Now he, Arash, goes his way; higher, and his body burns as if in a furnace. He goes; his clothes are gone, his ears sharp to listen to the way of the winds. He hears twice, thrice, that they call him by his name. He looks back and he knows that the whispers of soil are with him. He goes, for a while he hears no sound; except for a hidden cry, beating deep within his chest. And he turns his face to the mountain-top, to the clouds that are the wheels of Nahid.[12] And he sees pure Nahid, who passes through the sky, white like fresh snow.

■ The mountain, the mountain Alborz, to him – to Arash – says, "Ho, Arash! Ho, Arash! If thou desirest, if thou desirest, I will blow a wind pregnant with death to land on thine enemy. If thou desirest, I will create lightning that will burn everything to ash. But where art thou going with such speed? Thou art going to the highest of the heights, for the highest of the heights is a place for the lords of the sky. And but for them, and but for them, no one may reach that place."

And he – Arash – who is an entire man, says nothing and goes. To the highest of the heights, to the place for the lords of the sky, he – human Arash – goes, and his bow curved, his arrow straight, with him. The sky beneath his foot; the sky, the bearer of all clouds; the clouds full of rain; the rain, master of earth; and the earth, bed of grief; and he – Arash – the child of the earth full of grief, reaches the highest of the heights.

■ He – Arash – his bow leaning on the clouds: " – My mother earth, this is the arrow of Arash. He was a shepherd, compassion gave him a fiery heart. He has not held a bow, never, and he has never released any arrow. He never hurt an ant or set a trap. He was from those whose bread depended on the wind. Who is Arash? Who was unknown at dawn and now the eyes of the cosmos are upon him. A warrior whose most dangerous weapon was the shepherd's crook. An ignorant frontiersman who if someone were to steal his flock, he would still love the thief with his gentle heart and refrain from cursing or screaming. Who is Arash? A back-bent man full of his burden, carrying it all without complaint. I am the Arash that you knew, a man of virtue and piety. He was taught only to love, he knows not how to begrudge, but now, look at me, look at the thoughts in my head. Now I am in pain from a man who is close to me and far from me, a foul man – called Arash – who has infected me with his shameful name. He is standing on the other

---

12. **Nahid**   Rendered as Anāhitā in Old Persian, Anāhīd in Middle Persian, Anahit in Armenian, and Anaitis in Greek. The Zoroastrian goddess venerated as the divinity of "the waters" and associated with fertility, wisdom, healing, and war. She is the Iranian counterpart of the Greek Aphrodite and of the Babylonian Ishtar.

side of the earth on top of the summit, like a mirror in front of me, and his heart is my target. A foul man, so impure and disgraceful that they even prevent him from swearing or from passing the fire. I am Arash, who at dawn was ignorant and free, but now knows much from this world, and I cry loudly, 'I wish I did not know!'"

Now Arash, scared from his cry. In front of the endless sky – this silent sky – he, shaking with all of his limbs: "I rose from the soil but the soil has not risen from me. Once upon a time there was nothing but compassion within me, and now – my mother earth – I am full of hate."

And his scream becomes distant, until silent.

In this silence he closes his eyes. His body surrenders to the wind. His clothes are gone, he is naked, he takes the bow that was leaning on the clouds, he says under his breath, "Me – as I am – standing in front of you, I came to your refuge, and now you are the only one who knows who I am. So, be my witness."

And now he – Arash – whom compassion gave a fiery heart, he holds up his bow, a bow more curved than the back of the sky.

■   The earth rose, and the sky fell, Arash's feet on the earth, head to the sky, his arrow set in his bow. He – the human Arash – pressed his foot firmly into the earth, and Mehr[13] – who passed by the wheel of the sun – he went far beyond his throne, reached beneath Arash's feet. Arash took his bow straight with his forty limbs. He drew the bow and the clouds began to shake. He – the human Arash – drew the bow with all his strength, and the roar rose from the winds. And he, Arash – child of the earth – drew the bow with the strength of his heart, and sharp lightning struck. His bow bent and bent again, and loud waves from the sea. Arash's bow bent and bent again, and the earth shook fiercely. A roar coming from the heart of Alborz, and the fast sun stopped, and the seven skies tangled, and the color of the sky changed to that of the reddest wine. The clouds split. The rivers turned back from their ways. What lightning, what lightning! Alborz said, "How could I bear him on my shoulder!" And his tongue was flames of fire. And a roar rose from the beings of the cosmos, because on the highest of the heights Arash was not there anymore. And his arrow is going to the farthest of the far. And the clouds' mighty roars, mighty cries. And the sun hidden, and the sky invisible. And the people were shouting, "Arash will return, Arash will return." And that arrow was tall like a spear, and the spear was very tall itself, and the spear, that belonged to Arash, is still flying. And the winds are blowing to find it. It passed three mountains, that were standing on top of the sea. Seven plains full of flocks. Over many, many rivers. And five seas whose coasts were not found, from every sea another sea to other seas, and in the sea many waves. And three times the sun fell, and rose again. And three times

---

13. **Mehr**   Rendered as "Mitra" in Vedic and as "Miθra" in Avestan and Old Persian. The Zoroastrian deity of oath, justice, covenant, light, and the sun.

the storm appeared, and calmed again. And for three days the people stood at the foot of Alborz – that tower of the seven skies – waiting for Arash, the son of the earth, to return, but he did not return. And again, for seven days they stood, until he, who was a complete man, was to return, but he did not return in seven days. The searchers came with Hoomann, "We found the body of the Champion that the enemy ran horses over, and we found no trace of the Turanian encampments." And the arrow was flying, it passed the dry desert where no human was found. Over the green meadows of abundant grasses. Over the sky where Mehr turns the wheel of the universe and over those seas that Nahid has crossed. And the searchers who went looking for Arash returned; wrinkled brow, and hair white: "How can he return? He shot his arrow – that arrow like a tall spear – with his spirit, not with his arm."

And the arrow was flying. And the wind pursued it. And many horsemen of enemy and friend followed it, and they strayed behind it at the previous border. Beside a lone tree; big, brawny, bold, behemoth – shadowing. There was a bird sitting on that tree, croaking and singing; horsemen gathered around her song. Then the bird flew gently, to the clouds, until she disappeared. And the horsemen, at this sign, stepped off their horses and fell prostrate upon the earth. And the arrow was flying. Day after day, night after night; slaves who came back saw the arrow's speed, and hostages did too. The stragglers could not believe the plains they saw, this commotion was among the people who appeared from the back of the ruins. And everyone was talking about him; father with son, brother with brother, sister with sister, and woman with her husband. The passion arose, the legend of the arrow came from every mouth; from face to face, tribe to tribe, generation to generation. Until the universe is still, the arrow will continue to fly.

■ The sun offers light to the sky and to the earth, and it is beautiful at dawn. The clouds rain gently. Meadows are green. There is no harm. There is happiness, it is others'. And now Alborz; he is tall and his peak carries the sky. And we stand on the foot of Alborz, in front of us, enemy of our own blood; with a hideous smile. And I know the people who are still saying, "Arash will return."

Testament of Bondar Bidakhsh[1]

[for two readers]

I SAW HIM! I SAW! I AM SEEING HIM NOW, he who is being carted in an ass-drawn chariot; toward the zinc fortress! Six spearmen surrounded him on six sides. I asked him, "Art thou able to make one like this again?" He answered, "No more supremely." And I saw a glimmer in his smile. And I, who am Jam,[2] joined scream to scream, "So thou art able to make one like this again; though no more supremely? A chalice[3] like this; inside of which the span of the span of the world is visible? What will happen to me if a chalice like this falls into the hands of the demonic – through which they can watch me; how I am pondering, acting, and feeling? – Burn this knowledge!"

■■   Alas, zinc fortress that I made myself, now I am your prisoner, so accept me with a greeting! From the height of that peak, from that cloud-covered summit, watch me at your foot; broken and small-limbed, carry me toward thee, in an ass-drawn chariot! I, who without knowing, was building a prison for myself; from where there is no other way but death. Its doors are closed to the world, its cavity dark, its bottleneck tight, its ways devious; and corridors, nested deadlocks; I wish, yea I wish, there were a pinch of acuity from that chalice within my mind; that beforehand I could see this day within that chalice and craft a hidden path of escape for myself. Who is this who rose as mine enemy but for my blindness? – I must gaze further into my wisdom if he is as in battle with me.

1. **Bondar Bidakhsh**   The word "Bidakhsh" is a title that was employed in the first through eighth centuries. It has no direct English equivalent, but is similar to a marcher lord. The character Bondar Bidakhsh is an invention of Beyzaie inspired by a mythological character, Jamasp, the wise counselor of King Wištāsp, from *Ayādgār ī Zarērān*, a Pahlavi drama and one of the earliest surviving plays in Iranian history.

2. **Jam**   One of the most prominent figures in Iranian mythology, predating Zoroastrianism. In the *Rigveda*, an early incarnation of Jam is referred to as Yama, who is one of the first two human beings, alongside his twin sister, Yami. In both Indian and Iranian mythology, the figure is the son of the sun. In the *Avesta*, his name evolved to Yima, and he ruled the world in a golden age as a prototype of an Aryan king. With the aid of Ahura Mazda, he saves animals and the human race from a harsh winter by building a palace named Varjamkard. In Islamic literature, the figure is called Jamshid and rules a state where he is praised as the founder of a new civilization and as the inventor of many sciences. However, Jamshid becomes hubristic and vainglorious, which leads to his defeat at the hands of Żaḥḥāk. See Introduction for more background on the mythological basis of the play.

3. **Chalice**   The mythological chalice typically said to have been invented by Jamshid, though in this play invented by Bondar Bidakhsh. The chalice acts effectively as a crystal ball: Jam can observe the goings-on of the entire world by gazing into the chalice.

41

■   Here is the fate of the one who said nay! Even if he is a skilled astrologer; or a worthy counselor for each assembly! Wherever thou art pick a nail and write upon raw adobe, "I – comely Jam – friend of good people, and friend of domestic animals, and friend of fruitful plants – I, the one who is Jam – with the help of my sharp-eyed wisdom, I knew the enemy who was hidden from the eye though even I held him close to mine eyes!" Write down, "There is no fear for the unwise for they are their own cure. No – we must look deeply into knowledge to decipher its benefit and for whom? The knowledge that is not at my command, why should it exist? And if its harm is greater when it is within the claws of the enemy? And who is more cursed than the one who can grant like knowledge to us and to our enemy?" Hast thou written, little scribe?

Aha! I remembered from whom thou learnt this knowledge!

■■   I said, "Which enemy? O, king! O, Jam, for whom when ye are sitting upon a horse your enemy is windswept! And how do ye ponder I am accounting for them? The one who holds the crown of knowledge upon his head, how will he serve the corrosive and the unwise? Have I not spent all my years for this country; from youth until my time of white hair? Have I not spoken the knowledge of raising homes, have I not spoken the knowledge of knitting garments, have I not spoken the knowledge of cobbling shoes? Have I not made fine food from the essence of trees; have I not furnished the woodworker with axe and saw, and have I not given hammer and blowing fire to the blacksmith, and have I not proposed measures as *dang*[4] and *badast*[5] and *pangan*[6] and *kileh*[7] and *parasang*?[8] Have I not spoken the knowledge of well-digging, have I not brought water to the wheel and rope? And have I not broken fever from people with medicine; and have I not spoken the knowledge of stars? And have I not taken people as friends and have I not made you a wheel and while?"[9]

---

4. **Dang**   One-sixth of land, property, or objects.

5. **Badast**   The distance from the end of the thumb to the end of the pinky finger of a spread hand.

6. **Pangan**   A measuring bowl used to allocate water from a spring or aqueduct among peasants. One would place the bowl at a water source and measure the time it took to fill the *pangan*. This process would determine the amount of time allocated for each peasant to take water from the source.

7. **Kileh**   A measurement by which grain and flour are weighed, similar to an imperial cup.

8. **Parasang**   A historical Iranian unit of walking distance of ambiguous length, its closest European equivalent being the league. The unit has evolved into the modern *farsang*, a metric unit of six kilometers.

9. **Wheel and while**   A poetical way of referring to the fabled chariot of the god Mehr. Mehr's chariot-riding is often described as being akin to a wheel of fortune by which he controls time and fate. Bondar Bidasksh is being metaphorical when he suggests that he made Mehr's wheel/chariot for Jam; the intended meaning of this sentence is closer to, "Have I not done everything for you?"

■   And he is worse than ominous because each good the world brought he says he performed. And if he does not say so, people will think falsely that those things arrived from the knowledge he constructed; and they will say nothing of the *magus*[10] king! If he made many dishes from the base of milk – all decadent – and from plants fine stews – salty and sweet and hot and cold – who was it but Jam who brought *nabidh*[11] from the palm of dates, which is the head of all potation; and without this liquor does no one bear calm and happiness? And who made the order to construct the chalice and decanter; inside of which the wine for the friend is more delicious than the blood of the enemy? And who was it who brought out glass from the heart of stone; and silk from the cocoon? These were all from Jam; the wise king who has been called Face of the Sun.[12] And he, that headstrong one – Bondar Bidakhsh – that stubborn one; looked at me and said, "Burn all that ye wish, Jam, and do not burn knowledge!" – this crooked thinker, this posturer, this prattler, this wind-speaker! Nay, scribe, break the quill; and throw this adobe to the water!

■■   I said, "O, Jam! Ye, for whom six horses carry your wheel; I wanted nothing for myself from this knowledge. I brought about all this knowledge solely for the people; and today people everywhere see the profit of that knowledge. Then why is there nothing for me but bondage on hand and foot? Is it knowledge that has become an enemy to me? Nay; this bondage comes not to me from knowledge; it came from ye all. From he who looked conversely upon my knowledge!"

■   I, the one, throne-sitter; I, Jam – who made the world new when I placed the royal jewels upon my finger – I, yea, I who am Jam, I obeyed not the order of omnipotent Hourmazd[13] who commands, "O, come, comely one, be our prophet for the people!" And I told him it is enough for me to be Jam and to rule the world! I, Jam, who is from behind the moon and the sun, I told him it is better that I am this one; of whom people are coming to me upon their own desire; without my calling them; and they will read the Gathas[14] at six times, from the glow of the sun; and he – omnipotent Hourmazd – consulted me, Jam, in the manner of the world, to

---

10. **Magus**   Plural Magi; the only recorded title for clerics in western Iran during the Median, Achaemenid, Parthian, and Sasanian periods. In the Parthian and Sasanian periods, the term "magus" was used for Zoroastrian priests.

11. **Nabīdh**   A traditional fermented drink made from dates.

12. **Face of the Sun**   A reference to Jam having been born as the child of the sun.

13. **Hourmazd**   Middle Persian name for Ahura Mazda, the central deity of Zoroastrianism and the progenitor of the Abrahamic God.

14. **Gathas**   The central texts at the core of the Yasna, the Yasna being the primary book of Zoroastrian liturgy. The Gathas consist of seventeen Avestan hymns traditionally believed to have been composed by the prophet Zarathustra.

rescue the world from Ahrimanon![15] Hast thou written? – Write, "I, who am Jam, render the world from wars, and I gave a home and a place to the people. I gathered fine animals from everywhere; and I grew fine plants, and I subverted illnesses. Whereby the people grew in number; and they grew impatient from constriction; and their cries bothered mine ears. They told me tearfully, 'Ho, Jam, look! There is no place left in the world; soon we will crawl upon one another as snakes.' So I, who am Jam, I summitted Alborz – the whip in the fist – and I recalled Hourmazd, and I began to sing hymns of the new rites and of the old rites; and I whipped the earth, ho, earth! Grow vast for the people; and the earth grew vast. And the cry of joy of the people reached the empyrean sky. And up to three times the world constricted for the people; and I grew vast the world three times for them; with great prosperity. And all this I did in the name of the highest judge."[16]

██   All this was from knowledge. Wind, carry this speech, and mountain, bring back this cry, zinc fortress, thou clutchest it so it does not escape! Thou, oppugnant one, who now, like my knowledge – who laughs at me – clutches me! All these were from knowledge! All these were beasts and beast-tempered – riding on one another's necks – so that their armaments were the bones of brothers and of children; and the strings of their bows were the entrails of one another. Airyanem Vaejah[17] became contemptible under their hoof. Thereby I asked the worldbearer, Jam, to entrust the final battle with knowledge! Thus with the support of mirrors I threw radiance upon the enemy's eyes; I blinded them during the war so that they shattered. And the shine of a thousand suns burned their eyes and they fell down upon their skulls; and the earth became full of their stench and of their carrion; and those who survived escaped weeping and wailing and leaping toward ditches; shedding hoof; upon snout or tail; upon one hand or crawling; torn horn and broken nails; toward that dark side of the world; toward the rocky nothingness – such that no one saw them again! And so, with God's fire the earth became purified of their stench, people and flock calmed and the world rested. So, with the knowledge of vessels, I overthrew diseases; and I raised herbage and fine animals, and I taught people. Until the earth constricted; and people grew impatient. Jam asked for a remedy! – So I asked for the help of the people and with the knowledge of the soil drained the dissolute water; so that new lands appeared; and people planted seeds upon the land and the world flourished verdantly. And it happened thrice. And all this was from knowledge.

15. **Ahrimanon**   The plural of the word Ahriman. In Zoroastrianism, Ahriman is a malicious and evil force bent toward the destruction of goodness, the progenitor of the Abrahamic Satan.

16. **The highest judge**   Ahura Mazda/God.

17. **Airyanem Vaejah**   The mythological homeland of the early Iranians as mentioned in the *Avesta*.

■ I told them to write upon adobe and carve into stone and inscribe onto wood the tale of Jam, destroyer of the enemy; for from him there is abundance, joy, and fortune. Then for this victory I held many fetes and I made the new epoch. In the court, I appointed sentries to the bulwarks and the heights; with each sign they kindle fires and rotate mirrors, and send pigeons with letters. And I said, for the enemy-tempered ones, we must build a fortress of zinc so there will be no thought of beast-temperament among the people; so the people do not harm the shepherds and villagers. And each time they lift the insolent foot of battle, they remember what I did and they run away to the distance. And I said I wish that in all of Airyanem Vaejah, if I desire at any moment to know who is in pain, I may remedy his pain; and whosoever is broken I may mend his fractures; and whosoever is destitute I may salvage him; and whosoever bears a tear within his two eyes, I may erase his tear with promise and exuberance.

■■ Zinc fortress, I built thy roof like a night so that stars shine through thy holes. I built water-keeping reservoirs inside of thee. And upon thy land, I laid cooked adobe reflecting the number of days of the year. And I wrote on thy door, "May no one cross this door!" I made thee as the world. Twelve staircases as the months of the year, and each staircase with thirty stairs as the days of each month. I adorned part of those staircases bright green as in heaven and part of them dark and cold as in Hell; and thou art seeing within them people, animals, and plants, all carved from stone. And when I was building, all these in my mind were like a chalice within which the world appears. I am the one who is Bondar Bidakhsh, I was an astronomer to whom since childhood my father has taught a morsel of all knowledge; and when I came of age I followed all that knowledge. I looked upon the Chaldeans' parchment when I was a child, and I found their measures and their minds. And all that wonderful Babylonian knowledge upon cooked adobe I retained; from the prelude for when the water crawls and sleeps, to the phases of the moon and the radiance of countless stars in the rising of the aquiferous and in the germination of many verdant plants. From the ritual of arranging mirrors in the manner of the Egyptians; to the knowledge of amalgamation of roots and of elixirs, and the size of the galaxy, and those horoscopes and scales; and when and why is the sky full of light. From the preparation of pharmacopeias, and the construction of measures and weights, and the appearance of the figures of the constellations of the sky, to the mirrors of the light at night and the true chalice of the Indians. And the foundations upon which the Chinese made their magic lamp. So I pondered over a chalice in which the world appears; and I said, "This king has deserved it because he grieves for the world; to watch over the troubles of the people; from shepherd and hunter and troop and farmer and child and man and woman; and to untie those knots with his wisdom and to remove their bondage." And I worked for as many as ten years –

■   I asked him, "Canst thou make this again? This is mightily good; and all people are visible within it. Be upon us, we who are sorrowful of the world, look completely at this to see which sorrow can be taken from the world. Canst thou make this again?"

■■   I told him, "Ho, Jam, ye who are more radiant than the sun, this wore me out, my back was bent from this and mine eyes grew dark. I can make it; yea, but not so supremely!"

■   Not so supremely? – I replied to him, "Bondar, wise one, so thou canst make it! Which reward in the world is the exact counterpoise to this mirror? Ho, what is meritorious to thee? Tell me thyself; for we are small before thy knowledge!"

■■   Why did he melt poison into sugar? I told him, "Ye know me. I slumber late and rise early – occupied with my thoughts of people – very humbly! And I did this for your prosperity – with no prospect for myself!" He said, "So be it and so be it more so; why do we not make the prior year and the old world new? Why do we not celebrate, lay out a banquet, and blow the *sorna*?"[18]

■   Praised Mehr,[19] ho – fiery Mehr! What have I less than thee? Thou who hast eyes from above upon the earth; thou who art running the wheel in the sky – thou, Mehr, with a thousand ears, a thousand eyes; the owner of vast plains – what dost thou see that I do not see? Rivers? I am seeing within this! Mountains? This is Damavand,[20] this Alvand,[21] and this Karkas![22] And plains and hillocks? They are all here! And there are people; one by one with diligence. And demons all lie in their ditches; careworn and shuddering and furious! Yea, tell me – Mehr, on whom the light of the universe depends – what is it thou art seeing that I cannot?

■■   He told me, "Hast thou not heard of demons who hold much treasure under their heads yet are blind to see it? Perhaps thou wilt be in pain for a reward counterpoising thy pain is not in our treasure house and I wish thou dost not bring this knowledge where they give thee the counterpoising reward!" Yea – for I saw much profit in all this!

---

18. **Sorna**   An ancient Iranian wind instrument consisting of a long wooden or metal tube with several holes and played at feasts and banquets.

19. **Mehr**   Rendered as "Mitra" in Vedic and as "Miθra" in Avestan and Old Persian. The Zoroastrian deity of oath, justice, covenant, light, and the sun.

20. **Damavand**   Mount Damavand, a silent, volcanic, snow-covered peak of the Alborz Mountains in northern Iran. Damavand itself symbolizes the land of Persia in numerous myths and legends.

21. **Alvand**   A subrange in western Iran.

22. **Karkas**   A mountain chain located in central Iran.

■ He said, "Much profit?"

■■ I said, "Much profit?"

■ Yea, this is wonderful that with that chalice we can vanquish the septic and the hideous of the world; and erase from the country the uglinesses that left off the stench of the demon of demons and Ahrimanon. And look at this chalice to see where are sundry hunchbacks and broken chests and besprent teeth and soft bones and bald men and tettered men and squinting men and blind men and such men as these; and get them all out of this Var.[23]

■■ I asked, "Var?"

■ Write it down, "I – of the good flock,[24] Jam, possessor of open fields and vast pastures, I have a fortress – a garden; Var; where there is no way for ugliness and evil! And the finest selected people of any worthy kind are there; priests and scribes and warriors – artisans; whether farmer or whether shepherd or hunter; all thoughtful and healthy. They are within Var, the purest of my disciples; and also the finest of all finest; and the agile from each lineage and class; such as a *karnay*[25] player and a clapper and a throater; and bondmen and bondwomen good-looking and swift; fierce heroes and women with coy manners; they are all made-up and fine of face and fit! With treasures of gold; with the finest fabric and tools! And a pair of every useful animal I will bring over; and several and several of the finest plants; such as vine and anything fruitful! And the greatest flocks of the plain and the birds of the sky and the fish of the sea! I will be in this fortress; and infirmity and senility and death will be behind the door. This is my judgment: lion; king of beasts, and cow; king of domestic livestock, and eagle; king of those who jump upon the sky, upon wooden columns, they hold the roof of our court. And we on the throne of our own fortune are looking upon this revealing chalice of the universe at the working of the world. Tell me, ho, Mehr – who is the sleepless eyes of the world – what have I less than thee?"

■■ I asked him, "Ho, Jam, who converses with Hourmazd – did ye say, 'Var'?"

■ I said, "Yea, Var! How many times art thou asking? And there will be many people unhappy that there is no way for them to Var; and the world will be full of

23. **Var** According to the *Vendidad*, a sacred text of Zoroastrianism, Ahura Mazda informed Jamshid of a coming terrible winter, so Jam constructed Var, an underground cavern to house and protect a select group of the population, who would then repopulate the earth after the harsh winter was to pass.

24. **Of the good flock** This phrase is frequently used to refer to Jam in the *Vendidad*.

25. **Karnay** An ancient Iranian wind instrument.

gossip of all this. Yea, it is good if we discern what people have on their mind. And what the silent ones are pondering secretly and what warlords are carrying out; to which inhumanity are the troglodyte demons endeavoring; and from whence came this adversarial shout. Yea, thou performedst thy servitude greatly for me. It is good and it is better if thou burnest the knowledge! Lest one day tomorrow a little demon bears a chalice like this and upon it watches our acts and counts our army and distinguishes the sleeping from the woken; and while we close our eyes he would wreak havoc upon the world; and with a sudden raid disgrace Airyanem Vaejah. Yea, I became agitated with thee; that thy greed may deceive thee and thou mightest make a chalice like this for demons, so that they give thee equal recompense."

■■   The zinc fortress! Thou art my recompense of many years being burned on the light of knowledge! So make visible your rough paths for me. Ye eighteen thousand Babylonian adobe bricks, thirty thousand parchments of Brahmana,[26] and countless wood carvings of priests that I never stopped studying; when ye all conjoined together ye made a path that brought me to the prison of the zinc fortress! Demonic people for whom we made this fortress fitted are free; and who is not is me, who was told there is nothing meritorious to my knowledge! If only there was a path of escape for me, yea; and more than anything an escape from myself!

■   I have made ten hideaways from wood as ten fingers; and each time I hide thee, O chalice, in one of them; so the one who has planned to steal thee, his sanity shall be stolen! I will place the jewel on the same finger that is the count of that hideaway. Unless this is still not enough; for if a scoundrel sees my jewel on which finger it rests, he will now decipher in which hideaway the chalice lies. So come now, jewel that resembles a drop of blood; come and make their way lost. Come and be placed upon another finger; to mingle the signs. Now thou art hidden from all; but for my mind!

■■   With no doubt, he will see me within the chalice I made. Let him not rejoice in my suffering! So, ho, happiness, who is placed in heaven, lend a smile to my face! Let him know that I am carving this story into adobe! And not again; lest they throw this adobe into the water! – Think, man, that thou art in thine own prison; now they gave thee many days and nights to look at thy passed way. So, come, O, tolerant stone, who has a heart like glass; be my pen, and bear with me, do not break for my heart is broken. And O, raw adobe, who is heavy-hearted as I am; for I

---

26. **Brahmana**   Hindu commentaries on the *Vedas*, a foundational collection of liturgical Sanskrit hymns.

am entrusting thee with what happened – embrace it tightly, till posterity receives thee. Mayst thou not erode as I have eroded; mayst thou not crack and mayst thou not open holes over these elusive words, which are being carried as a gem by the wind, so that they escape from thee swiftly as swift wind; as bird from branch and life from body; not as I for whom there is no escape from this heavy-heartedness. Yea, with no doubt, he will see me through the chalice that I made; so let us now begin the testament –

■   I am me – I; Jam, the king, king of people, and king of countries; son of my father and my father and my fathers. I am he who, till it has been so and it has been, has performed many great deeds indeed; and I lined up all of these deeds on the hard crest of this enormous mountain, so that they will be testaments to my greatness. I am the one for whom there are patrons from the six corners of the earth, and my command will be valid over eight countries! And I did everything in the name of the Creator. And the world would not be this world were not I, Jam, sitting to adorn the world! Nay, scribe, stay and desist! – for he gave me such a bold response, yea, but not so supremely; he spoke of time beyond, not of time past! Had he not made another chalice beforehand, and is it not with him? Ho, chalice, hurry and show what he is doing, for until I know I will not be at rest! This is the mountain and this is the zinc fortress and this is him! I saw him! I am seeing him! There is little with him in the fortress with which he can make a chalice. Unless he has a hidden home within that wizard fortress; hidden from thine eye, ho, chalice! He may get whichever servant he desires. What do we know of what is happening within the guards' minds? And if he uses his hand for magic, how will they escape from his magic? From that magic which is hidden in the glory of gold! – Did he carry no gold with him? – Come, thou who wast his student once upon a time and today for thy fortune thou art a scribe for my secrets; leave writing and go be his servant; be with him to know his secret. On the first day, go to him like a priest who has divorced his heart from the universe, who has heard of the fame of this chalice and desires to gaze into the galaxy through this chalice. Another day, go like a merchant who owns much and who has heard that all bazaars are visible in this chalice and wants to buy it with gold. On the third day, like a demon man-devourer with a secret hoof and a shrouded horn, go near him and offer him the kingship of demons if he makes a chalice like this for thee. And on the fourth, go to him like an enchanting woman with a covered face who has heard of the chalice of magic and who wants to gaze through this chalice with coquetry to show her face and know there is no one fairer than she. So I should not see thee standing here shocked! Go and go sooner; and set aside no tricks! And if thou seest any chalice with him, raise a flag of the color of blood onto the fortress so that I may find a solution!

██   Thou who art reading this writing, be vigilant; for the day harmed no man; and see how men harmed the day. I was a man – my name lost upon the world – whom my father taught the duty of knowledge; and said it is profit for the people. And I was like a porter bull who carries several thousand pieces of leather parchment of the multitude upon a chariot and knows nothing of them, I knew not that it profited no one but with harm! I remember the day that the earth was full of the corpses of murdered demons, and with overuse, drums of chaos lost their shouting and melee. For this victory all became happy but me! I, from above, looked upon murders. So I went to my corner and closed the doors to myself and I spent many years on this chalice for its beneficence. And if one day they are going to judge me as to whether this chalice yields benefit or harm, will either I curse or pity myself; praise or despise? If in the mirror of my knowledge to profit someone they harm another!

█   Nay! Nay! Nay! I sent him to the zinc fortress and this was not enough! What would I do if the pupil were to become flatterer of the master and would perform servitude and he would take him on his side and with the help of each other they would make a new chalice? – Nay! The remedy for me is his death! Come; ye be those kind people who return mine escaped sleep to its place. Hasten and assail and look not at your back unless with his head! I wait for the moment when I, with a broken heart and a tearful eye, hear the report of his death with mine ears; and your silent witness will be his torn corpse that speaks a hundred languages with the mouth of his wounds!

██   Make haste, Bondar; haste – of this testament that thou art making! What dost thou know of tomorrow? Or of today itself? If he is as thou knowest him, then thou knowest very well what is now going on in his thoughts. Yea; that is it! It follows me, the order of my death! What is the better song for the ear of the world but the song of forgiveness that the *magus* king sings by himself upon my death? Be swift as the way is full of riders; of intractable steeds, whose anger drives them to peel the earth. Of the visible dust who stood up to the sky; and in the eyes of the fiery way only the shine of blades fights with the raised darkness of the soil brought by the wind. Only the neigh of sundry rebellious arrows is my justice-seeker; which remains unheard amidst the moans of the soil pounded under the hoof, and the clinking of the armor of defiances. Yea, the valiant and the swaggerer come one by one to avenge my bloodshed. Yet firstly who is this? In front of myself I am seeing the face of the student of myself; or someone hidden in his face! Art thou not the one who learned writing from me? What is this that thou puttest aside the refined garment of the scribes and puttest on thy body the coarsest of the most wretched sycophants? Perhaps thou camest to see with thine eyes how I am carrying this load of pain? Or how works the inescapable circle of the zinc fortress? – However, think not that there is no escape from there. Yea, there is: with the aid of such a friend as thee; who will let me wear thy clothes and step out from the door that they open for thee! Or perhaps thou camest to see what appears as the hopeless people of the world? I will tell thee; yea, I appear only as myself! So a salutation to thee, that thou camest properly; and thou saidest not how thou came? And what is this with thee? A covered object that appears as a bowl of blood. Is this not a chalice within which my cut head with unseeing eyes will look upon Jam? Or a chalice with which before death I will wet my throat? This secret, whatever it is, remove the curtain from it! – Ho; then this is the world-revealing chalice that I made!

■　Sentries made cries that the bloody banner upon the zinc fortress flows in the wind! So a salutation to my messenger who opened the secret! What a chalice is this; and did he make this beforehand or inside the fortress? I must look at it; where is my chalice? – Perhaps I should go to the zinc fortress with mine own foot! Lest anyone receives the chalice to become someone; or a leaping demon in his flight in the sky, his eye sees that world-revealing chalice and he throws himself down upon it and with his deception and anger and tyranny steals it. Where is my chalice?

■■　Come, O chalice, thou for whom I gave up all I had; very soon my life as well! Let mine eyes for the last time look upon thine eyes who see the world. Ah, I saw it! I saw! This is the land that I loved dearly; and these are people – with their efforts – who deserve better; and this is the court of Jam, of which the lion and the eagle and the cow are holding; and this is him. What art thou showing me; what I am seeing – Jam has become insane? From losing the chalice?

■　Ah, why is there nothing more within this chalice but my twisted tilted face? This looks as that and this is not that. Who did this and how did it get here? And where is the real chalice? Or the jewel is fooling me and the chalice is in another hideaway? I will open all of you one by one and I will check you all – where are you, and where is it? Ten chalices as this; all with my twisted tilted face – and all pity me! May I not lose my wisdom! These chalices in which everyone sees himself! Did I not order this trick myself; for he who has eyes following the world-revealing chalice does not distinguish that one from one similar? No – where did I put it and with whom did I entrust it, and why? Is this the chalice that withers and is silenced and stopped whenever its creator is harassed? Chalice, my world-revealing chalice, where is it? A unique gem that appears as the sleepless eyes of the sun! Oh, Jam, ye have grasped a treasure without affliction and thrown it away! And how do ye look at the work of the world anymore? And who is as he who could build one as that chalice? Nay, I should not shed his blood! Not before he makes me another chalice!

Ho, come, the obedient are on the path; get ahead of them! Whatever courage ye
have put on the field and without hesitation charge and arrive before them! Bring
Bondar Bidakhsh alive. The bloody banner flows in the wind; then for him there is
a chalice; and for me the world-revealing chalice is lost.

■■   I saw him! So this is it; those quick with the decree of my death; and those
slow with the decree of my life! How soon that which I thought did happen. Do
I escape? – Where to? – Dost thou know there is no way of the zinc fortress but
death? And for me the only escape of death is this raw adobe upon which I write
my testament?

■   Undoubtedly someone somewhere is seeing me within the chalice. Do not
lose thyself, Jam! Ye are the king of kings, the head of Magi! Why did this worry
come to thy head? Someone is counting the wrinkles on my brow; and reading the
quivering of my lips; and my thoughts! Should I go toward the left or the right?
Should I slumber or set? Should I go or stand? Should I chant or sit with wine or
raise my hands? What should I do so he thinks not that I am afeared?

■■   Ye are afeared, Jam! Ye are also as us! Now ye know what it is like to be
under the gaze of others!

■   The one who stole this chalice – that menacing one, that demonic one – who
grasped it; he now knows where he is. And he knows of those quick with the decree
of his death; and of those slow with the decree of his life. And if I, with mine own
body, charge toward the zinc fortress, he knows that I am going with mine own
foot. He knows that he has a chalice hidden that he sees himself within, and also
me. Alas, there should be a chalice for me, so I can know within whose hands is the
chalice that I lost.

■■   Aha, I am seeing thee little by little in the chalice of my thoughts; and I am
seeing what thou bearest in thy mind! Thou toldest thyself that the king of crowns
will come and take this chalice; and for this service thou performedst for him, he
will always be grateful to thee; he will venerate me for this secret hidden chalice;
and he will restore my life and my position; and forever with complaint he will
murmur that demons and magic stole that first chalice. And through this one, he
looks deeply for that one and does not find it; and he may think that Hourmazd
did this to him for retribution. And perhaps it is all in my head, not in thine. So tell
me, what is in thy head? Thou, why didst thou do this? And since I am the only
witness who is aware that both chalices are one and the same, the chalice that thou
stolest, what willst thou do to me for fear of that day when I will speak the secret

and when I will speak what is true? Tell me, what is behind that smile the chalice does not see that I can see?

■   Woe if they arrived early and killed him! Woe if they arrived late and the blade passed over veins! And if late; mine enemy bears a chalice and I do not! All those cursed ones, those who know not of the gem, whom I was seeing within the chalice; wretched and wicked and garrulous; sharpened teeth and raised tail and avaricious; as dogs around a full chalice, they stole the chalice from the claws of one another to see Jam the demon-slayer who lost wisdom cheaply! Where can I find thee, chalice; where should I search for thee? Woe if they laugh at me; that I cannot tolerate! Be broken, thou, chalice, if thou art not mine! These beasts have their sights on me yet I have not mine on them! The demons who are each of them are many demons; Ahrimanon masked as men and men worshipping Ahriman; of whom their food is sludge. From their gaze, where should I go, for the universe is full of their sneer? Yea, perhaps I should make a fortress in which I can hide myself from eyes; yea, a garden like Var!

■■   Wouldst thou like to tell him this is another chalice that Bondar Bidakhsh made in the zinc fortress? And didst thou fly in the wind the bloody flags to make him aware? Why? – Thou thoughtest thou mightest make my life longer? Or shorter? Didst thou not hear he said to burn this knowledge? Or perhaps something else happened, and until the moment whence I am making a chalice as this I am alive; as a skylark in prison who until he sings he is in prison and if he fails to sing he is dead. Or wouldst thou like to tell him that this is a chalice that wast made beforehand? And what is the answer if he asketh, why hast thou hid this from me? So reveal the secret and tell why thou performest this servitude and for whom.

■   Ho, Jam, what was this thought? What, whither, whence, and wherefore? For if he cares to bestow the chalice upon demons or to make one hand with the enemy, he will have done this before he presented you the chalice! Why did ye imprison your friend and indulge your enemy? And why for him who always speaks to your face did ye send a mediator so now ye know not which speech comes from the mediator and which speech comes from him?

■■   Oh! What happened to the shame of the days? When was it whence I pondered that a disciple of mine would look at me churlishly and say to me, "Master, it is better for you to abandon this testament and all ye do for ye are attributed to death; and whatever is your secret in making this chalice, leave it with me so that I may live my life!" When did it pass through my mind that thou, shameless, reviling, evil-gazing one – who wants to steal the chalice from Jam and the life from me –

would tell me aggressively, "This knowledge that ye threw away cheaply ye should leave with me so I can sell it costly. This magic of the demon and the fairy that ye mixed together! That with its help, I will build wealth and status, and I will raise my head among grandees, and I will place my foot upon the ninth wheel,[27] and fill my bowl from the chalice of heaven of the sky, and grant the throne of fortune from Shid and Jam!" He says all this but he does not say whether he speaks his own speech or whether he was ordered to speak; to test me. Or perhaps an arrow toward two targets: of which on one side thou raisest a flag of servitude to him; and on the other side, thou pretendest I have my life from thee and thou seekest from me a reward counterpoised to my life! Know that I am indigent and that nothing in this world is with me; but the secret of this chalice; if I teach it to thee, from then on, yea, into thine eye, evil-eyed one, my life is not worth living and that is mine end; and then thou, ungrateful one, will sit in my place and will perform the servitude that I did not perform for him for whatever he bears in his mind; and from him thou wilt ask for costly rewards and high positions! High positions, yea; no higher than this place that thou art in now! No higher than this zinc fortress! Or wouldst thou say I stole the secret from the master and made this chalice by mine own hand. Ho, say, this trickery is not within thy thought? And thou didst not know that in doing this, thou art pouring thy blood into a jar;[28] when he desireth another chalice from thee and thou canst not build one?

■   What are ye saying, Jam, reside on your throne; drink wine and smell pleasing scents and daub oils onto your body? Why should I sit down – nay! Saddle my thunder-steed and bring my war garment with one hundred sorts of edged blade. I – who am Jam – with my body I straddle and with the beating hoof of my windlike white steed, I shorten the long way to the zinc fortress. Hold a parasol of cloud in front of the sun soon; and before that – why do ye say it is already late and was all for nought? With all haste dispatch a messenger like the smoke with my jewel; which like a fired arrow surpasses the wind; and also fly a wind-feathered pigeon, with my command, to break the paths of the sky that lead toward the zinc fortress; and tell that Jam breaks his command!

■■   I share this secret with thee so that knowledge does not leave the hearts? Yea more pleasant; since life is tied to a hair, I tie it to another, so it becomes a solid string. And nevertheless, nay! How should it be known what will come out of that chalice which ye will build with knowledge? If someone bears that chalice, wherein he looks at the sufferings of the people and can do nothing, what is the benefit

27. **The ninth wheel**   The highest part of heaven in Zoroastrian liturgy.

28. **Pouring thy blood in a jar**   To "pour someone's blood into a jar" is a Persian idiomatic expression roughly meaning "to make everything difficult for a person."

except that his suffering increases? If someone bears that chalice, who handles everyone and who looks into the chalice to see the affairs of the dissatisfied and becomes dissatisfied with them, what can come from this chalice but the soaking of a laugh in blood? If tomorrow and tomorrow they take a peasant out of his house and hang him, wilt thou not say it was the chalice and wilt thou not curse me? A curse upon me and may they not call my name with goodness if I do share and do not take this secret with me to nothingness! A curse upon me, for I ruined my life in making the best thing for the benefit of the best of the world and nothing blossoms but bane.

◼︎   Why should they lower the bloody flag even when it is aflame? What is the secret but that our thought became ash and flew to the wind? So, the one my courier found, is it of the same sort as the ten chalices I have in the hideaway? I wish broken the legs of those who are further out, and faster the legs of those who are behind, and that my messenger passes both of them, and that my pigeon arrives earlier than all; I who am Jam, want Bondar Bidakhsh alive.

◼︎◼︎   I see them, swift passersby following the command of my death! Roaring and foaming at the mouth; at the foot of the zinc fortress; upon white horses, sweaty, roaring, and restless; all with their drawn swords, their nostrils shaking from their rage and roar and they see nothing upon the soil but boiling blood!

◼︎   What is the benefit of being Jam when I lose the chalice? Nay, let it be lost; as if it were not! I, before this, without this world-revealing chalice, was also Jam. So why should there be a place for sadness? Be still Jam; whatever ye are under the gaze of demons! Write upon raw adobe, "They spoke nonsense; not one ever saw that chalice! This knowledge has not been seen among us! The unwise one who was bound to the land of demons, there, saw a mirror bent and toyed with; and from that mirror he devised a mad story. This was a fable that a fruitless person recites; all enchantment and canard, all thought and speculation!

◼︎◼︎   Now they are behind the door! No bird arrived and no messenger knocked on the door! Dost thou leave me to them that they with the most irritated curses kill me through stampede? Is there no kinder death in thy hidden dagger? The hidden dagger thou couldst draw if thou desiredest yet did not; the dagger with which thou thoughtest thou couldst frighten me and force me to reveal the knowledge of this chalice? Yea, I see them; wide-eyed and with wrinkled brow! With the cry of roaring and roaring and the breath of shouting and shouting, the doors were open for them. And if they are the following ones carrying the command of my life – thou tellest me; is that not more ruinous than my death? To push me to Jam's foot; and ask me to construct another chalice for him? Nay, I will not tell thee this knowledge! Nay! Let the knowledge die whenever it is within the fist of the death-ponderers; for they will make all benefit into harm. And before death I will knock this chalice upon stone and we, both of us, will break together! Alas, a salutation to thy kindness that is hidden behind rage and dagger! Now I have received my reward with thy razor; the reward of life given for knowledge! I give thee something of my pain in return for the kindness I received from thee; yea, remain and write the story of this chalice upon the parchment and read it to the people; so that they will not say we lacked this knowledge.